CHERISH LIFE!

CHERISH LIFE!

**FULFILLING A DESTINY IN GOD
WHILE LOSING
THE ELECTION OF 2008**

A BIOGRAPHY OF

SARAH PALIN

AND FAMILY

By Janice Leasure Woodrum

PREPARING THE WAY PUBLISHERS

Copyright © 2008 by Janice L. Woodrum. All Rights Reserved.

No part of this publication may be reproduced, stored in a retrieval system or transmitted in any form or by any means, electronic, mechanical, photocopying, recording, scanning or otherwise, except as permitted under Section 107 or 108 of the 1976 United States Copyright Act, without the prior written permission of the publisher.

PREPARING THE WAY PUBLISHERS

411 ZANDECKI ROAD
CHEHALIS, WA 98532 USA

Janice Leasure Woodrum

Cherish Life!
Fulfilling a Destiny in God While Losing the Election of 2008
A Biography of Sarah Palin and Family

ISBN 978-0-9821642-4-2 (Paperback)

Printed in the United States of America

Unless otherwise noted, all Scripture quotations are from the New International Version of the Bible. Scriptures are taken from the HOLY BIBLE, NEW INTERNATIONAL VERSION Study Bible, 10[th]Anniversary Edition, Copyright © 1995, Zondervan Corporation. Copyright 1973, 1978, 1984 by International Bible Society. Used by permission of Zondervan. All Rights Reserved.

DEDICATIONS

This book is dedicated to:

Trig Palin

Second son of Todd and Sarah Palin, created by the hand of God and gifted for very special works in "such a time as this" for today's world.

and to

Tough Chuck ... Darlin' Charlie

Role-model for Trig Palin, friend and hero of Sarah Palin.

ACKNOWLEDGMENTS

A very special thanks to my husband, Dave, who loves me, works with me, believes in me, and encourages me to attempt and accomplish more than I think I can. Without his vision and ongoing encouragement, I would not have finished this task and honor. You're my hero. Your editorial expertise is also priceless. My dear friend Carol, thank you so much for all your help with research.

Thanks to author daughter, Amber, who critiqued and proofed this book, helping me also with technical details. I'm grateful to James Wrigley, who graces the cover along with Governor Palin and baby Trig. You guys look great!

And thank you Governor Sarah Palin for standing firm on the Word of God, and governing with honesty, integrity, and perseverance. Thank you for believing in and acting out your strong convictions for the sanctity of human life, and for the cherishing of these "good and perfect gifts from above" – your new son Trig, your soon to be born first grandchild and countless others.

You are indeed my first and only heroine!

TABLE OF CONTENTS

Copyright	…………………………………	4
Dedications & Acknowledgements	……………	5
Table of Contents	…………………………………	6
Who Am I	…………………………………	7
Prologue	…………………………………	9
Introduction	…………………………………	11
Chapter 1	The Issue of "Life" ……………	19
Chapter 2	Incubator for a Leader …………	33
Chapter 3	A Modern Day Deborah …………	49
Chapter 4	The "Real Man" in the Background…	63
Chapter 5	Family Matters …………………	77
Chapter 6	Track's Tracks …………………	83
Chapter 7	Bristol's Bravery ………………	89
Chapter 8	Willow's Wistful Ways …………	95
Chapter 9	Piper's Play ……………………	105
Chapter 10	Trig's Triggers …………………	113
Chapter 11	Great Rewards …………………	123
Appendix	…………………………………	135
References	…………………………………	149
About the Author	…………………………………	152
Other Publications	…………………………………	153

Who Am I?

I am under 45 years old.
I love the outdoors.
I hunt.
I am a Republican reformer.
I have taken on the Republican
   Party Establishment.
I have many children.
I have a spot on the national ticket
   as Vice President with less
   than two years in the
   Governor's office.

Did you guess?

I am Teddy Roosevelt in 1900.

- Forwarded anonymous email

PROLOGUE

The following is a portion of a letter from Carol, a long time Juneau resident to her close friend in another area who had asked her opinion on Governor Sarah Palin, the newly chosen running mate for Senator John McCain as he ran for President of the United States in the 2008 election.

Hi Sherry,

Hopefully, you received my forwarded links to our little dynamo of a Governor, Sarah Palin. While I have never met her and cannot claim to any intimate knowledge of her, her choices speak for themselves. It is apparent she has made choices like one who is intimate with the ways of God.

Her pre-knowledge that the fifth child of she and her husband of twenty years, was a Down's Syndrome baby, long before the due date, did not sway her decision to carry this Gift from God to his birth day. The fact that she found herself in a gubernatorial position when she knew this... the fact that it may have been easier and certainly not looked down upon by so many of our day didn't sway her.

She has stood for righteousness (or, now more commonly called "integrity"), whether in the PTA, the Mayoral, or Gubernatorial positions. She doesn't appear to care who it is that is making decisions that are unworthy, she doesn't appear to fear for her own reputation. Even when the injustice is being done by the Goliaths around her, she doesn't seem to notice their size! She reminds me of David... No coward here.

You can look for her on almost any major platform that stands for family, and dare I say Christian values, and find her solidly standing in the middle of them. From what I read, she is a member of a thriving church in her home town of Wasilla ... She says of herself that she is a non-denominational Christian. Hmmmm ... I've said that too!

For what it is worth, my initial response to her nomination was one of great joy and excitement. This was shared with all the co-workers in my office as we skipped work to follow the acceptance speech shown live on Foxnews.com over my boss' computer. I was fighting back the tears. We all just felt like celebrating... It gave me a renewed hope and excitement for this election.

It is a thrill the see her there, and I hope profoundly, that the faithful in the place of prayer will surround her with their prayers. That her family will be so hedged in by the Lord's mighty warriors that they may play in safety. That her son being deployed September 11 will remain safe, that her daughters and her husband will continue in their support of their warrior wife and mom, that her newest little one might be such a blessing, that his life will show forth the glory of the Lord.

So, in 'not-so' short, we are so pleased. But as probable sisters-in-the-Lord, let us lift up her arms!! Amen! WAHOO!!!!!!

Love you,

Carol

- This email was a forward of a forward of a forward to countless people, that thankfully ended up in my "In Box" during the course of this research. I am so very grateful for her candid and eloquently shared opinion.

10

INTRODUCTION

This Alaska citizen's opinions are applauded with a resounding "Amen" from my little office in Washington State, but in my heart I know there are multiplied hundreds of thousands who could also put their resounding stamp of approval on this well-worded affirmation. Recently I have made a very disappointing discovery. It's funny that in all my 60 years of life I had never awakened to this fact before.

In my entire life I have never had a heroine!

I had studied about Biblical heroines: Ruth, Esther, Deborah, Mary and others. But I'm not sure I had even looked for one in our modern day personalities.

When my son, Kit, was just a small preschool boy we had dinner in a special restaurant in Tacoma, Washington. At that time Geraldine Ferraro was running for vice president, and we happened to come upon her in the lobby of the fairly new Tacoma Sheraton Hotel. Kit had flaming red hair and the characteristic cowboy boots and shirt he always wore in those days. He was hard to miss. Suddenly she turned around as he approached her without fear … and she actually bent to shake his little hand. He didn't know much about a race for president or vice president, but she was obviously someone famous, and it thrilled his little heart and those of his sister, daddy and me. A local newspaper photographer even snapped their picture for the next day's paper!

I was thrilled that a woman had finally made it to this point of acceptance and responsibility. But her ticket, her record, and her character make-up didn't ring true in my mind or heart as things I wanted to emulate. Now, about 30 years later, I have considered much more about whom I want to become by God's grace working in my life, and I know something more of the Scriptures ... what does God look for in a leader, especially a female leader? The standard seems somehow even higher for a *female* leader.

During this presidential race of 2008, a question was brought up about whether Sarah Palin could keep up her responsibilities to her family. Then one newscaster had the courage to bring up the obvious double-standard of that question: "Had anyone asked the question whether Mr. Obama had kept up the close ties with his little daughters during the hectic race from city to city to shake one more hand and deliver one more speech?"

A funny story circulated in the news that went something like this. "Sarah Palin and the Pope were riding in a gondola in Venice or somewhere with water streets. His elaborate papal hat blew off in the breeze and floated some meters from the boat. He became agitated, not knowing how to retrieve it, and not knowing how to exist without it. Sarah said to him, 'Don't worry; I'll take care of it.' She got out of the boat, walked over to fetch the hat and return it to him in the boat. The next day's newspaper headlines read, 'Sarah Palin can't swim.' "

Yes, I am convinced the standard is higher for a woman, and perhaps the complete "job requirement" is actually greater. As I watch my daughter, a physician specialist, struggle to get even a deep breath over her eight month pregnant belly, I become certain of it.

And as if I needed more confirmation of this opinion, I found a recent piece in *Disney Family Entertainment*, entitled "Election Moms: Sarah Palin, her secret to success." (http://family.go.com/entertainment/article-594385-election-moms--sarah-palin-t/5/)

It reports this: "We don't sleep much. Too much to do. What I've had to do, though, is in the middle of the night, put down the BlackBerries and pick up the breast pump. Do a couple of things different and still get it all done."

I'm not sure I could ever come up with that level of dedication. But then again, I never really had a real live heroine either. I'm not sure I even thought consciously that I needed a heroine. Maybe I had been content to cling to the ones I had discovered in the pages of the Scriptures, not even expecting that there might be such a real live person in today's world.

Then suddenly things began to change, to my amazement and excitement. As the announcement was made by Senator McCain of his running mate in his race for the White House, and the drama started to unfold, I began to see the unveiling of a genuine model, the real deal ... the heroine I had been unknowingly waiting for all these years! As a strong disciple of Jesus Christ and a minister/missionary, I can finally enthusiastically support this one who doesn't seem to compromise sound Biblically-based values. One night a few weeks after her début into the race with John McCain, my husband and I were watching the news, and I made the excited proclamation to Dave, *"She is my heroine!"*

I had been following her carefully, examining what she said and did as brought forth by TV interviews, coverage of various speeches, and reading commentaries available through the media. I was looking for something I could emulate in my own life, while at the same time wondering if I would find a fatal flaw that would disqualify her from that semi-pedestal position in my mind. But though some of her "humanness" was exposed by the inevitable news coverage she got in the best of times and the hardest of times, she continued to stand up to the rather lofty standard I had developed after decades of studying Bible characters. She remained my heroine right up to the end … the final moment of acceptance that they had not won the race for the White House. It didn't change my opinion of her. In fact it has strengthened and solidified it.

The months since she entered the race have sped by, and there has been so much to observe and discover in this ruggedly outdoorsy and yet breathtakingly beautiful and poised professional woman. The time flew by too quickly, and now the election is over, just over a few short weeks ago. And I find I'm not ready to let go of the hope, not ready to see my heroine disappear once again into the imagined cold and dreary Governor's Office way up in Alaska.

Perhaps in taking a little deeper look into the woman who so graced the podium of first woman Republican Vice Presidential Candidate, and the family behind her brave race, I could somehow solidify my memory's vision of this heroine. Perchance I could also discover pearls of wisdom as I look deeper into their lives, and compare some of their attractive features and stances with those of Biblical heroes and heroines in similar historic life situations.

I invite you to join me in a quest to hold on to the memory, and rekindle a greater hope for the ordinary American family, the "Joe the plumber" worker, the valiant parents and siblings of special-needs children, those children themselves, the young women with difficult life decisions to make, those who invest their energy and life resources into fighting for LIFE ... and women everywhere who just need a heroine.

Janice Woodrum

CHAPTER ONE

THE ISSUE OF *"LIFE"*

I knew by the Spirit of Christ within me that an older Christian leader was speaking the truth in discussing briefly the upcoming presidential election. The real issue from God's perspective, he said, is life – human life ... not economics, nor the war in Iraq, nor health insurance in America. It is not one of these – but life, life of the unborn and unprotected. One president and vice presidential pair would protect the life of innocent unborn persons; the other pair would protect a woman's right not to be inconvenienced by pregnancy for nine months out of her entire lifetime. For after all, there are millions of sterile families crying to adopt babies, aren't there?

This personal perspective rang true to my mind, my heart and my spirit. For I knew from God's perspective the issue of respect for human life, or the practice of sacrificing innocent human life was the major issue on God's heart for who should rule as president and vice president of a great, free and powerful nation such as ours. After all, aren't the rights to life, liberty and the pursuit of happiness foundational in our country?

At least I thought they once were …..

Then came the day of the election. As my husband and I met for Bible study and prayer as we do every morning, we both took time to close our eyes and pray quietly and individually to God for a few minutes. Soon in my mind's eye I saw the words *Obama* and *nation*. Then as I watched, these words gradually came together to become one word – *Obamanation*.

Then I read the word and spoke it in my mind, and I gasped out loud, "Oh my God!"

At the same time Dave was seeing a vision as he prayed. He saw a giant tsunami coming as he stood on a beach. He was terrified, but could do nothing to stop it – he could only watch it come closer and closer to shore. We pondered the meaning of these spiritual events as we left our prayer time and went about our day.

A little later I wrote an e-mail to a girlfriend of mine who is an intercessor. I explained my unusual vision from earlier that morning. As I prepared to send the letter, the computer did the automatic "spell check." It recognized my word *Obamanation* as incorrectly spelled, and suggested a correctly spelled word. You guessed it:

Abomination.

I stared in disbelief at my computer screen. The program itself had verified the thought I had when I saw the word with my eyes closed. To have an Obama led nation in alignment with a liberal Congress would most assuredly perpetuate the abomination of abortion in the land. Your consciousness is shocked that I should use such a word. But God used it in the Scriptures to denote the things that were abhorrent to Him, the things that would require His judgment. This current demonstration of disregard for human life would subsequently evoke judgments from God upon America, in addition to those we've seen in the last few years in the form of hurricane Katrina and other devastating hurricanes and tornadoes, rampant uncontrollable forest fires, severe damaging floods, crop failures, other destructive weather patterns and economic meltdown in America.

A sense of impending darkness and mourning crept silently over my spirit as the day of the election progressed, and I could not seem to shake it. Then in the evening came the verdict of the American public, as one newscaster after another on the TV channels discussed a virtual "tsunami" of votes coming in from certain states for Senator Obama. And soon it became perfectly clear that we would indeed have an Obama nation.

As we watched the pronouncements of President Elect Obama, I discussed with my husband how perplexed I was about Sarah Palin, the pro-life Republican Vice Presidential Candidate. She had over these months become my heroine – standing up against abortion even when it was costly and inconvenient for her. News sources have told the story that she knew before birth that her baby son, Trig, would be born severely handicapped with Down Syndrome – yet she chose not to abort him. And at the ceremony of her acceptance of the V.P. nomination, her young daughter Bristol, and Levi Johnston, the father of her unborn child, were allowed to share the limelight of the event with Governor and Mr. Palin as loved and supported family members; not as ostracized outsiders who made a foolish and unfortunate mistake.

As we considered the election results, I shared my sense of disappointment with Dave, saying, "I had so hoped she would be a modern day Esther or Deborah, coming into her V.P. office and working to reverse Roe vs. Wade, or otherwise halting legalized abortion in America.

But now that won't happen. I don't understand why God would set her up for this position and then not allow her to be elected. "Lord Jesus, we so want to understand this from your perspective," I prayed with Dave.

I was so disappointed and confused I couldn't even watch on TV the speeches by Obama and McCain, but went to the bedroom to be alone and pray. Then finally the lights went on in my mind and spirit. I thought of a phrase Dave, a minister and missionary sometimes uses:

"Before God brings a judgment on a situation, He first provides a clear standard of truth and righteousness, so that His judgment is justly administered."

I thought of the anti-abortion movements we were aware of or had taken part in personally over past years: The Cause, (24 hour prayer and worship movement within site of the National Capitol in Washington D.C.), Prayer for "Life" at the Justice House of Prayer in Kansas City, the monthly Kansans for Life meetings when we lived in Kansas, the red wrist bands reminding us to pray several times a day for an end to abortion and for revival in America, and many others, including most recently a large intercessors gathering in Colorado attended by a friend who is a fervent intercessor.

Some have labeled this slaughter of 50 million innocent unborn since 1973 the greatest holocaust of all time. And yet it continues unbridled. And every day that the innocent ones are murdered pulls more and more judgment upon our country and the people in it. The intercessors have cried out, wondering, "How long will God withhold His judgments for these sins," and also sensing that some judgments have already begun upon our land.

As the lights began to come on in my mind and heart, I considered that God is concerned about the issues of the presidential campaigns, such as economics, the wars in Iraq and Afghanistan, health insurance and so forth.

But nothing stirs His heart with compassion, concern, pain and even anger as does the legalized slaughter of the innocent ones – which is nothing less than an established altar to gods of convenience, selfishness, self-determination and murder. The ramifications are no less significant than those of King Manasseh who sacrificed his sons in the fire to the God of Molech, and whose sins were greatly responsible for the exile of God's people to Babylon (2 Chronicles 33:6).

I believe this issue of abortion was foremost on God's heart as the citizens of the USA went to the polls to vote on November 4, 2008.

But before that vote, it seems to me that God raised up a standard for the USA and for the nations, for surely our events are viewed by the entire world by means of today's technology.

His clear, clean, unmistakably stirring and complete standard was this:

This hockey-mom come Governor of Alaska, come Vice Presidential Candidate of the USA will be viewed in history, if we have eyes to see, as the standard God raised up to mercifully (one last time before the critical vote) remind His people, the citizens of the USA and the watching world, of His standard of respect for the sanctity of human life at any stage of development. Her public demonstration to the world seemed to crumble the arguments of those upholding rights to slaughter the innocent unborn such as:

"This unplanned and unwanted pregnancy will …

…interfere with my opportunity to finish school."

…impair my ability to seek a professional career."

…shame my family and their reputation."

…be a burden to myself and society."

…be a risk to my personal health."

I don't think I'll ever forget the images in my mind of Sarah Palin on stage accepting the nomination as Candidate for Vice President of the United States of America. And in the audience were her husband, Todd, and her daughters, Bristol, Willow and Piper, taking turns lovingly holding and caressing precious baby boy Trig, with Down Syndrome. They were sitting next their oldest son Track and the oldest daughter, Bristol's fiancé, Levi. This couple chose to face the crowd of the world, displaying her family's love for them and their respect for human life at the highest level. Then came the announcement of their son Track's deployment to the Iraq war, demonstrating with his life the valued qualities of respect for life and liberty.

Sarah Palin, her family and their choices seemed to dwarf the arguments for abortion, as they defied them in their very life choices in front of a watching world. As this woman had earned and accepted this honor, an honor at a level never surpassed in the political history of America, she also became an unmatched standard of holiness for the U.S.A. and the world. She ranks with the Biblical heroines of Esther and Deborah who stood up to powerful forces to save their people from destruction.

As I pondered and prayed about all these things, it seemed to come into clearer focus why she came to this place of V.P. candidacy, and there fulfilled an incredible destiny for her life, even though she and presidential candidate McCain were not elected. There's a bigger picture ... **A PICTURE OF GOD'S JUSTICE TEMPERED WITH GOD'S MERCY.**

God's justice would rightly require judgments upon a nation whose legislative and judicial leaders would not only legalize the slaughter of the innocent unborn, but protect it for 35 years to the untimely destiny of 50 million of them ... down the drains of abortion clinics and even hospitals though the U.S., or even going up in smoke in crematoriums such as the one in Wichita, Kansas designed and constructed specifically to dispose of the results of "late term and partial birth abortions," that is near-term babies who could have taken their first breaths and lived their own lives, had not their brains been sucked out with a suction tube on their way through the birth canal.

Would not God need to judge such a thing, even as He did those in Old Testament times who sacrificed their sons and daughters to the God of Molech? (2 Chronicles 33:6)

But I believe, even after this abomination before God for so many years, God may have said to Himself...

"I'll give them one more chance – a chance to turn away from this abomination of human sacrifice before a full 40 years of it have gone by." (Forty years being an historic Biblical measurement of times and seasons, especially in the Old Testament).

So in the magnificent magnitude of His mercy, He raised up, or perhaps even "set-up" Sarah Palin as His chosen vessel on the face of the globe to become one last shining beacon to the world, to demonstrate how possible and admirable it can be to overcome the arguments for abortion. But also to demonstrate this stand, at a cost to herself and her family – a stand for the holiness and righteousness of God's commandment, "Thou shall not kill." She took a stand for the rights of every citizen of the U.S.A.

He seems to have set up for all the world to see, the most wonderful combination I can imagine of a woman who is beautiful, poised, funny, dedicated, principled, industrious, a team player, an astute and effective politician – and at the same time just a normal "hockey mom" American woman, loving and serving her husband and children, protecting even the weakest of them from an untimely death ... even to her own hurt.

God put a multi-faceted and many CARAT diamond of a woman in front of a watching nation and world as His one time CARROT to entice, if possible, a nation away from its abominable path to self-destruction, and toward a path that could lead to a lasting remedy and removal of the impending judgments He would have to bring upon future generations of Americans.

As spiritual leaders such as Dutch Sheets began in the days following the election to make some meaning of it all and some predictions for the future, the inevitability of an increase in God's judgments upon America came forth as a universal pronouncement of truth. But as it unfolds, America can not say it wasn't warned, and can not say there was no strong alternative presented. On the contrary, the life and message of this dazzling diamond all but blinded America with the truth that young women and older women can cherish life and keep their dreams and ambitions, while at the same time doing what is right in God's eyes and turning away the curse that abortion can bring to their lives.

America is without excuse. God has presented a clear and attractive alternative by a pro-life platform and a full-life lifestyle for the world to see. God used a presidential election to take a vote of the decision-making adults in America. It was a vote for life or death.

Life didn't win, and death will reign in many different manifestations in America as a result.

What a destiny! God used a simple "hockey mom" to take the pulse of the most powerful nation in the world at what will prove to be one of its most decisive turning points in history. This was a power-full destiny, perhaps even more important than decisions she would have made or works she may have done as vice president. She fulfilled a profound destiny in God, even though she lost the election. **Destiny fulfilled in the presence of defeat** – what a dichotomy of thoughts. What a picture only a sovereign God could reproduce.

What about you? Has your life contained unmet dreams, unfulfilled hopes, unfinished victories you worked and fought hard for? There is yet a destiny saved up for you by God in the midst of one of these, or perhaps because of it. I believe Sarah's destiny will help you discover a pathway upon which to find it.

This book will let us take a closer look together at the making of a woman of destiny with glimpses of her life and her experiences that trained and developed her for local and governmental offices, her family – her impact on them and their impact on her, and other influences and events that led her to this place of destiny. We will look briefly at the lives of several Biblical characters facing similar experiences and challenges, and glean from them pearls for living successfully in ways that please God, even amidst adversity and disappointment. And finally, the life of Jesus will be discussed as the supreme example of a life fulfilling the greatest destiny of all history, amidst the apparent defeat on the cross and in the grave ... and the victory of His resurrection.

CHAPTER TWO

INCUBATOR FOR A LEADER

Sarah Louise Heath was born in Sandpoint, Idaho on February 11, 1964, about the time of the performance of the class play in my junior year of high school. Sarah came into the family "classroom" of Chuck Heath, a teacher, and Sally Heath, a school secretary. She sometimes went moose hunting with her dad before school, and some sources say she can even "field dress" a moose now! As the third of four children, she watched several other young "teachers" of a sort from day to day.

As a family they regularly ran 5 km and 10 km races. This training may have helped her develop endurance for her basketball career. But soon some of her strong personality traits began to boil to the top as she served as point guard and captain of Wasilla High School's state championship girls' basketball team.[1]

Her desire to come out on top, a strong competitive spirit, seemed to surface as she earned the nickname "Sarah Barracuda" preparing for and playing in the state championship.[2] Later in her political career this nickname would surface in a court of much greater dimensions and ramifications.

Interestingly, she also is said to have a strong Christian faith from early youth and a history of regular church attendance. In high school she was head of the Fellowship of Christian Athletes chapter at her school. During her college years she won the Miss Wasilla Pageant, then finished third in the 1984 Miss Alaska Pageant, at which she won a college scholarship and the "Miss Congeniality" award."[3] The early spotlights didn't seem to blind her vision for greater things.

In 1987 Sarah graduated from the University of Idaho with a communications-journalism degree.[4] There may be political science teachers still around who are busting their buttons in pride at what they helped to mold into the clay of this young girl's make-up. (It sure gives me a sobering thought to hold onto as I prepare and teach Sunday school lessons and mission field messages to pliable young lives today).

34

During this campaign I've wondered where she came up with that poise ... the ability to speak with her measure of self-assurance and grace. But in recently viewing some clips of her broadcasting performance in 1987 as sports anchor at KTUU, an NBC affiliate in Anchorage, I could see that these two years were a good training-ground for being in the world's spotlight today, answering some of the hardest of questions one could ever anticipate. She was also a sports reporter for the Mat-Su Valley Frontiersman.[5]

One little squeeze here and another push there; and the model of poise, self assurance and fluency of speech began to take shape within the theatre of public life. I ponder the query arising in my mind: "Were these just happenstance short term jobs, or more little twists of the hand of the Master Potter, who inspired the apostle Paul to write the words, 'And we know that in all things God works for the good of those who love Him, who have been called according to His purpose?'" It makes me quiver in the sobering thought of the influence I could be having with the casual remarks I make to my children and grandchildren, or "children" of another sort in frequent letters winding their way through cyberspace to India and Pakistan.

The ball really seemed to get rolling for Sarah's life, as she married Todd Palin in 1988; their firstborn, Track was born in 1989; and in 1990 oldest daughter Bristol was born.[6] She was off to a running start with the beautiful family we see today! But these little blessings didn't seem to deter her a bit from pursuing her destiny in public life. For in 1992, concerned about local taxes and how they were being spent, she won a seat on the City Council of Wasilla, Alaska, a town with a population of under 10,000; and she served in this capacity until 1996, when she was elected Mayor of Wasilla.[7]

It was a very natural progression, it seems, for a relatively "small town" girl with a strong personality, who really cared about her community and wanted to make a difference for the better.

It makes me think of Artie, a woman from my older sister's graduating class, who a few years ago was elected mayor of a town a little smaller than this – Paola, Kansas. In owning the town's only taxi company, she meets and escorts lots of people to their destinations within this pleasant burg. And with open ears she takes the pulse of the community's politics, commerce, spiritual institutions, health care opportunities and much more. She had been a leader in their high school class, even a rebel of sorts; and now she is influencing in a major way one of the finest communities where I have had the privilege to work and do my weekly shopping and other business. I think I'll make a mental note never to despise small beginnings ... we never know where they may lead, perhaps to a street called Pennsylvania Avenue.

One discovery I made recently about Governor Sarah Palin told me something that may have seemed like a small beginning, but became a huge impact into the very scrupulous character of this prominent political figure. I stumbled upon this goldmine glimpse of her sharing briefly at the Wasilla Assembly of God Church where she had attended.

Web (Link.brightcove.com/services/player/bcpid766638341)

In this clip the pastor there revisited an earlier time when Mayor Sarah Palin had been at the church. "The Mayor is here ... she is a disciple of the Lord Jesus Christ *before* she's a mayor."

And then speaking of her as Governor, he said, "Governor Sarah Palin is the 'real deal.' She loves her husband like nothing else; she loves her children like no-one else; she loves the State of Alaska ... she wants nothing but the destiny fulfilled for the State of Alaska." He then spoke about Pastor Paul Riley who had led Sarah Palin to the Lord, baptized her, and helped her get discipled – a long and strong history of faith.[8]

I marveled at the implied impact of the decision she had made earlier to be a disciple (a follower, an imitator, a subject) of the leader and teacher, the Lord Jesus Christ. It seems to have molded her character as a wife and mother, and also that as a leader in local and state governments.

It was once prophesied of Jesus Christ in Isaiah 9:6-7: "For to us a child is born, to us a son is given, and the **government will be upon his shoulders**. And he will be called Wonderful Counselor, Mighty God, Everlasting Father, Prince of Peace. Of the increase of His government and peace there will be no end. He will reign on David's throne and over his kingdom, establishing and upholding it with justice and righteousness from that time on and forever."

And it's comforting to know that the weights of the **government upon her shoulders** will be shared under the yoke of this one spoken of so majestically by the prophet Isaiah. For the Lord Jesus invites and encourages us in

Matthew 11:28, "Come to me, all you who are weary and burdened, and I will give you rest. Take my yoke upon you and learn from me, for I am gentle and humble in heart, and you will find rest for your souls. For my yoke is easy and my burden is light."

Some critics in the recent political campaign debates have minimized the responsibilities and the outcomes of her tenure as Mayor of Wasilla. But in reviewing her history in this office, I was favorably impressed with her activities and accomplishments.[9] To name just a few, she

- Defeated three-term incumbent mayor John Stein on a platform targeting wasteful spending and high taxes.

- Orchestrated needed reforms in local government offices.

- Created the position of city administrator, reducing her own salary by 10%. (Later the change was reversed by city council.)

- Followed state legislature events and supported certain issues at the state level.

- Polled community members by phone on a regular basis for their personal opinions.

- Cut property taxes by 75%, utilizing an existing sales tax for revenues.
- Tapped municipal bonds for improvements to roads and sewers, and increased funding to the Police Department.
- Oversaw new bike paths for the community.
- Procured funding for storm-water treatment to protect freshwater resources.
- Reduced spending for civic buildings.
- Won re-election in 1999 with a 74% vote.
- Was elected President of the Alaska Conference of Mayors.
- Joined with local communities to lobby for federal funds, securing $27 million for public works in the Wasilla valley area, including a youth shelter, a transportation hub, sewer repairs, and a rail project to a nearby ski resort to increase city revenues.[9]

I wonder if Sarah Palin's heart for her community and for the small business owners in America was in part born out of her experience from 1988-2007 as co-owner of a commercial fishing operation, and also of a sport vehicle rental business from 1994-1997.[10] And, oh, did I forget to say that daughter Willow was born in 1994?[11] Looks like even then Sarah managed to handle a professional life and family as well, like so many of today's women. If she can do it, then maybe I can ..... And along came the sweet and charming little Piper in 2001.[12]

Then came the giant step forward in the game of life, as in 2002 she ran in the Republican primary for Lieutenant Governor of Alaska, coming in second against four experienced public figures.[13] Looking at her in her gubernatorial position today, it makes me think, "If at first you don't succeed, try, try again!"

In 2003 Governor Frank Murkowski appointed Mrs. Palin as Chairwoman of the Alaska Oil and Gas Conservation Commission, giving her a "shoe in" to the arena of energy policy in which she plays an influential role today.[14] This seems to have been a major "shoe up" into greater landmarks in her political climb.

So far we can see that she wasn't afraid to start small, not despising the day of small beginnings, and never forgetting those today in their places of small beginnings and "small potatoes" businesses or political positions. From my point of view, I begin to see how each of these early positions seemed to play a part in the larger platform developed in her stance as U.S. Vice Presidential Candidate. The words of the Apostle Paul ring through my memory again, as he said once, "Be very careful then, how you live – not as unwise but as wise, making the most of every opportunity, because the days are evil. Therefore do not be foolish, but understand what the Lord's will is" (Ephesians 5:15-17).

Some other opportunities seemed to help craft her into the woman she is today. A strong sense of right and wrong, fair and unfair, finally had to flesh itself out in real life battles against attitudes, attributes or ambitions that don't line up with the plumb line of integrity upon which she had built her life and political career.

So in 2005, we see she butted heads with the big boys, and filed an ethics complaint jointly with Democratic legislator, Eric Croft, against Gregg Renkes, Alaska's Attorney General on charges of financial interests in a trade deal, causing Renkes to resign.[15] Also in '05 she appeared in an ad promoting gas pipeline plans, at odds with Governor Frank Murkowski and the interests of powerful oil companies.[16]

And finally in August of 2006 she challenged this now not-so-popular governor in the Republican Primary race and won.[17] At the age of 42 Palin became Alaska's first female governor, the youngest governor in Alaska's history. [18]

Wasting no time, in February of 2007 Governor Palin initiated plans to construct a 30 billion dollar pipeline to transport natural gas from Alaska's North slope to the lower 48,[19] already winning points as a "team player" with sister states not so well endowed with natural resources. In August, 2008 Governor Palin signed House Bill 3001, authorizing the State of Alaska to award TransCanada Pipelines a license to build and operate a pipeline to transport natural gas from the North Slope to the continental United States through Canada, with an estimated project cost of $26 billion.[20] This gas line will be the largest construction project undertaken in the history of North America.[21]

These interests and political landmarks have paved the way for her to be a strong voice in the race for independence from the merciless iron grasp of foreign oil that we struggle to get free from today. There is no more relevant issue on the table today, as a country such as Iran fails to even get a hand slap while it continues to enrich uranium, towards potent nuclear weaponry; despite impotent U.N. warnings not to. And at the same time Iran continues to export massive oil stores to the West. Governor Palin sees a way to break free from the "mad" man, A<u>mad</u>inejad, of Iran, and other bully nations who expect that we are putty in their oily hands.

Top priorities that Governor Palin set for herself include development of natural resources, education and workforce development, public health and safety; as well as transportation and infrastructure development. Ethics reform is also high on the list, and an early legislative action was to push for a bipartisan ethics reform bill, which she signed into action July, 2007, calling it a "first step" in her determination to help clean up Alaska politics. [22]

With the soaring fuel prices earlier in 2008, development of oil and natural gas resources is high on her list of priorities, including the pipeline project from Alaska to the lower 48 states.

Her trip to Kuwait was an important step of experience into international issues, as she visited the Khabari Alawazem Crossing at the Kuwait-Iraq border. There she met with members of the Alaska National Guard at several bases, feeling the pulse of our involvement in the Iraq war. From there she returned home through Germany, visiting injured U.S. soldiers in hospitals there.[23] This was an excellent way to help her "count the cost" of the principles our troops have been fighting for in the military theatres of Iraq and Afghanistan.

This experience surely must also come to her mind as she remembers and prays for their son Track in his service there in Iraq.

In Governor Palin's time in office, she has also taken strong measures to keep costs down and the state budget in line. She succeeded in selling the jet Murkowski purchased against the wishes of the legislature,[24] and has fought to develop the economy of Alaska, reducing dependence on federal funding. She has requested less in federal funding each year than her predecessor Frank Murkowski requested in his last year.[25] Please see the Appendix for her November, '08 speech to Republican governors outlining some of her other ongoing goals and aspirations for herself and the other governors.

With these responsibilities and opportunities under her belt, sooner rather than later she was on the launching pad for much loftier things. To quote "Milestones: Sarah Palin" from the New York Times, November, 2008, "Governor Sarah Palin, Senator John Mc Cain's surprise choice for a running mate, has worked to cast herself as a *reformer*, taking on former allies in her own Republican party to become the first woman and youngest person to win a place in the Alaska Governor's Mansion."[26] Also, "polls taken in 2007 showed her with a 93% and 89% popularity among all voters, which led some media outlets to call her 'the most popular governor in America.' " And her poll results in September 2008 were still at 68%.[27]

This strong gubernatorial history was a good spring-board for the final rebound to the top race in the world today – the race for President and Vice President of the United States. And race she did with energy, strength, endurance, integrity, poise, spunk, and wisdom beyond her years ... wisdom beyond even herself, I would dare to say.

A favorite picture in my mind is one of Sarah Palin standing before her church family, with hands folded in prayer, receiving the intercessions of spiritual leaders as they sought from the Lord Jesus Christ the wisdom, direction, strength and guidance for the most weighty season of her life to date. She was considering prayerfully an upcoming role as a U.S. Vice Presidential Candidate – a role that after a specific time of favor with the American public ... followed by a few missed heartbeats, could catapult her into the most powerful chair in all the world – the swivel chair of the Oval Office in the White House, Washington D.C.

That did it ... that snapshot in the church fellowship sealed her in my mind and heart as my heroine ... one who would come to submit her will and highest aspirations to the One who sits "in the heavenly realms, far above all rule and authority, power and dominion, and every title that can be given, not only in the present age, but also in the one to come" (Ephesians 1:20-21). She demonstrated that she is not her own, but bought with the purchase price of the blood of Jesus Christ, the Supreme Ruler of the Universe. And if elected, I believe she would submit the greatest of decisions into His hands, His lap and His heart. For the wisdom from above is "first of all pure; then peace-loving, considerate, submissive, full of mercy and good fruit, impartial and sincere. Peacemakers who sow in peace raise a harvest of righteousness" (James 3:17-18).

Now that's the kind of leader I want, when America seems to be going down the tubes into deeper and deeper levels of depravity. That's the kind of heroine I can look up to. Yes indeed!

CHAPTER THREE

A MODERN DAY DEBORAH

Still glimpsing our heroine out of the corner of one eye, let's take a look backward to see more closely a wise and brave woman of old, Deborah, the leader of Israel. In Judges Chapter 4 we read that the Israelites had done evil in the eyes of the Lord, and He allowed them to be cruelly oppressed by a vast army under the leadership of the commander Sisera. "Deborah, a prophetess, the wife of Lappidoth, was leading Israel at that time." She received a strategy from the Lord and said to the son of Abinoam from Kedesh to take a thousand fighting men and lead the way to Mt. Tabor. She stated that she would lure Sisera, the commander of the army oppressing Israel, with his chariots and his troops into the Kishon River valley, where the thousand fighting men could overtake the army of Sisera. But he refused her proposed plan, saying, "If you go with me I will go; but if you don't go with me I won't go."

She submitted to his request and went with him, while at the same time prophesying again and informing him that by using a different strategy he would not get the honor of defeating Sisera, because the Lord would give Sisera over to the hand of a woman.

So Deborah went with him to approach Sisera and his massive army with nine hundred iron chariots, a different way. At precisely the right time Deborah revealed the Lord's will for the battle and said to him, "Go! This is the day the Lord has given Sisera into your hands." So he went down Mount Tabor and engaged Sisera's army, defeating them all, except for Sisera who abandoned the battle and fled on foot.

He fled to the nearby tent of Heber and his wife, Jael, who was in the tent at the time. She invited him in to rest, and at his request for water she gave him milk, a place to lie down, and she even covered him up. (Is this where we get the notion of warm milk at nap or bedtime to help us sleep?) He warned her to stand guard, and in his exhaustion fell fast asleep. Then she crept up quietly and ran a tent peg through his temple and into the ground on the other side of his head, killing him. She got the credit and honor for defeating the enemy army's commander.

In Chapter Five we read what is known as *Deborah's Song* about the events of the battle. She says in verse 2, "When the **princes** in Israel take the lead, when the **people** willingly offer themselves – Praise the Lord." And similarly in verse 9 she says "My heart is with **Israel's princes**, with the **willing volunteers among the people**. Praise the Lord!"

Let's look for a moment at the days Deborah lived in, and consider a few of her character traits and abilities behind her political and military success in those days. Judges 4:1-3 describes how the Israelites had once again ignored God's commands and "did evil in the eyes of the Lord. So the Lord sold them into the hands of Jabin, a king of Canaan, who... cruelly oppressed the Israelites for twenty years; (then) they cried to the Lord for help." As a prophetess, Deborah was able to discern the times and seasons of the Lord. And she knew the ways of the Lord. She knew the Word of the Lord, and His stated precepts, whereupon He would bless Israel when they obeyed His commands, and bring punishment or oppression on the people when they "did evil in the eyes of the Lord." Her key for action was that though the people had been oppressed for twenty years, "they cried to the Lord for help." Her prophetic unction moved her to take action, for the time was ripe for deliverance from the enemies of Israel.

If we look back 20 years in America, we get to 1987-88. I believe the Lord was beginning to raise up an army of praying believers, who were disturbed by what was becoming of America. With prayer coming out of schools in the '60s, and abortion legalized in the '70s, American society was beginning to come apart at the seams in the '80s. We could see deterioration of the integrity of the family unit; there was escalating violence everywhere, especially in the cities, where there were "drive-by-shootings", robberies and other explosions of lawlessness. Societal standards held high for centuries in America began to corrode and crumble. Then in the late 80's God began to raise up a praying remnant, with eyes that saw what America was becoming and hearts to hear God's heart about it. My husband and I joined with countless others in what we called "Concerts of Prayer for Revival and Spiritual Awakening" in America in numerous cities across the nation. Intercessors (concerned Christians with an anointing for prayer) began to call city-wide, county--wide or state-wide prayer meetings, with a focus on repentance for the attitudes and actions that were offending God, and a hope that the tide of lawlessness would be turned from America. We knew then and still believe that God's hand is moved by prayer. In 2 Chronicles 7:14 we read that

"... if my people, who are called by my name, will humble themselves and pray and seek my face and turn from their wicked ways, then will I hear from heaven and will forgive their sin and will heal their land."

In Israel God had raised to a place of influence and authority a prophetess and strong leader who could hear the people crying out for help, and could also hear His heart of empathy for those with repentant hearts, willing to turn away from the sins that had offended a holy God. She seems to have heard that the time was ripe for God's deliverance from the hands of their oppressive enemies, and she was able to convey the heart of God into the circumstances and events of the time.

God spoke a strategy to Deborah; she heard it and delivered it to the leader of Israel's armies. In this strategy, Deborah was willing to lay her own life down for the sake of the name and reputation of God, for the people of God and for the land of God. To go out as the "bait" to lead the army of the enemy into an ambush put her in an extremely vulnerable situation, which could have easily cost her life. She didn't ask for more courage from the leader of her army than she was willing to demonstrate herself. But it seemed to be too much of a challenge for him, and he needed her to go with him into the battle. So she was willing to make adjustments in the plan to work "in team" with the commander and the nation's army, in order to subdue the enemy of their land.

Deborah was truly a "team player," willing to put others first while remaining in the background. "My heart is with Israel's princes, with the willing volunteers among the people" (Judges 5:9). We see this same "team player" spirit in Sarah Palin. She threw her hat into the ring with the "big boys," the men who were at the helm of the Republican party, and linked arms with a powerful senator, John McCain, to stand up for righteousness. She argued the issues with candor and uprightness, holding her own valiantly in debates with those of diametrically opposing standards and ideologies. She held her own, so to speak, with other powerful leaders in this country, not ashamed of her record of demonstrated leadership from citywide to gubernatorial levels of influence and responsibility. She voiced strong standards of righteousness that she would support if granted the second in command position in the powerful nation of America. Surely her heart and influences had been with the "princes" in high positions in the land.

But even more amazing to me, is the way Sarah Palin demonstrated, as did Deborah of old, her stand of like-mindedness, empathy, appreciation and support of the "willing volunteers" of the land. Deborah had sought the Lord for the strategy that would give the entire army of Israel the best chance to defeat the army of their oppressors, with the least loss of life and resources. A large part of her day-to-day responsibilities had been to listen to the injustices or disputes that arose amidst common men living life together in community, offering the resolutions that she sought from the heart of God's wisdom for each situation. She was not aloof from the common man, but closely involved with the issues that concerned the people; and she was directly responsible for the proposed solutions. This was a part of her heart, and I believe a part of her song, for the "willing volunteers," the common people of the land.

I believe it was also Sarah Palin's heart of appreciation for the state of the "Joe the plumbers" of America's communities, as well as for the countless volunteers who had worked in the trenches of the huge campaign machinery for the election.

I saw a video of her at work a week following the election. She was back at her post as Governor of Alaska, and as such attended a caucus of Republican Governors of America. In her address to this group, she made mention of some of the events of the race for President and Vice President of the United States of America.

I quote from this address: "But far from returning to the great state of Alaska with any sense of sorrow or regret, we carried with us the best of memories and joyful experiences that really do not depend at all on political victory. For years to come I'm going to remember all the young girls who came up to me at rallies to see the first woman having the privilege of carrying our party's V.P. nomination, and they inspired me ... with one or two extra hurdles in front of us, in front of these young girls. I feel that we've got this mutually responsible relationship now, these young girls and me, where we're going to work hard; we're going to be stronger; we're going to be better, and one day one of them is going to be president, because in America there will be no ceilings on achievement, class or otherwise, and if I can help point the way for these young women, or inspire them to tap into their own gifts and talents and strengths to find their own opportunities ... well it is a privilege."[28]

As I heard this part of her speech, I couldn't help but think of their young Bristol, now facing the extra hurdle of an unwed teen pregnancy. In spite of that, their Bristol was blessed to have a mom and dad who stood beside her in allowing and even inviting her to stand beside them at perhaps the most important moment in their lives ... the ceremony for her acceptance of the Vice Presidential nomination for the Republican Party. She is one of those common people in America, alongside thousands of other young girls experiencing the same situation ... a girl with the uncommon courage and fortitude to cherish life, that is to honor the life of the unborn child within her as much as she honored her own life ... an uncommonly courageous act in today's world where abortion is the easier of the two choices.

It is the easier, but also the deadlier, both for the helpless tiny person within, and also deadly to the soul and spirit of the mother, who will carry with her the guilt of having taken her own child's life. And it will plague her mercilessly for the rest of her life, unless of course she comes to the Savior and burden-bearer, the Lord Jesus Christ, for His mercy and forgiveness for even this crime against the most innocent of persons. Praise God for the Christian crisis pregnancy counseling centers whose primary goals are to help meet the immediate concerns of pregnant women needing support, and also those needing some assistance getting out from under the tremendous mountain of guilt often present when one has had an abortion.

With a heart to help these girls "tap into their own gifts and talents and strengths," Sarah Palin's heart will also be turned towards her own daughter, Bristol, who will be tapping into God's gifts and talents and strengths for new mothers, as well as perhaps a professional career of her own one day.

Among the other "common people" Governor Palin recognized along the way in her speech to Republican governors, she remembered "all the people along the way who said that they were praying for us; they were such a strength and shield of prayer warriors."

Then there were the mothers of men and women in military service overseas, as she commented, "I remember the Blue Star Moms, and the special bonds we share with our loved ones away at war; I'm going to remember all the veterans of war and the former POW's that I had such an honor of meeting and hearing their stories ... and America can not forget. And we must honor and respect these men who have sacrificed so greatly for us ... and have such a love of country and need to be heard today."[29] These servicemen and women are the "willing volunteers" of our day, ready to sacrifice so much ... and readily recognized and appreciated by the mother of one of them.

And last but not least, she said, "I'll remember the working people of this country who put their faith in us; the folks who run our factories and grow our food and teach our children and serve us in uniform, those who came out on the campaign trail also to say that they had a lot of hope for the ideals that we were representing in our ticket. And I remember folks like "Joe the plumber" who spoke for so many, when "Joe the plumber" remembered and suggested that taking more of our families' and our small businesses' hard-earned money stifles the entrepreneurial spirit that grew this country into the greatest country on earth...... I'll not forget guys like "Tito the builder." He recently became a U.S. citizen, running his own construction company now. On the trail he was telling us so proudly, 'Yea I was born in Columbia, but I was MADE IN THE USA.' This is the land of opportunity. And to see every day hard working Americans who we would meet ... and again such a comfort we had knowing that we're not the only ones believing in America being the land of possibilities and opportunity."[30]

Like the prophetess Deborah of old, Sarah Palin's heart is with the "willing volunteers among the people. Praise the

Lord!" (Judges 5:9). And yet, as she spoke these words to a room filled with successful governors that day a week after losing the presidential – vice presidential race in America, she commanded an atmosphere of gratitude and respect among them for such an exhausting, brave and valiant struggle on behalf of righteous ideals held up by their party, especially those of the innocent unborn.

CHAPTER FOUR

THE "REAL MAN" IN THE BACKGROUND

What can we say about the man behind one of the most powerful women in America today? What did his beloved say of him? In front of all the Republican governors she said, "...along the (campaign) trail it was my husband Todd who was my right hand..."[31]

This man Todd, who has many achievements and trophies of his own, assumed the place of honor and service at the right hand of this powerful woman. It makes me wonder what kind of "stuff" this man is made of, who gladly takes a "helper" role alongside (dare I say) the most popular woman in America for a season. He must be pretty secure, self-assured, and not at all threatened by her position or political clout ... a strong leader in his own right.

Let's see what she said about him. "Among his many winning qualities is the gift that he has of optimism and just thankfulness in all situations that he finds. Going forward,

I'm going to count on those qualities a little more even because of course there was a disappointment after a loss of a national election like that. You run the race to win! I was kind of relying on Todd with that optimism of Todd and the thankfulness in all situations, and I'm certainly going to be there with him along those lines." [32]

I believe Sarah is saying she is going to follow his lead, because he has the stronger suit in his hand when it comes to thankfulness in all situations, and in keeping an optimistic attitude even when things get tough. I think his buttons must have popped a little, as he heard her laud among the other governors his strengths in such an enviable character attribute as an "attitude of gratitude."

This attitude reminds me of that of the Apostle Paul, who wrote to the Philippians reminding them to "in everything, by prayer and petition, *with **thanksgiving**,* present your requests to God" (Philippians 4:6). And then a little later in verses 11-13 he said, "…I have learned to be content whatever the circumstances. I know what it is to be in need, and I know what it is to have plenty. I have learned the ***secret of being content in any and every situation***, whether well fed or hungry, whether living in plenty or in want. I can do everything through Him who gives me strength." The first chapter of this book clearly states that Paul is in prison at the time of this writing. Certainly, it would require a great deal of personal character to be content with life in prison. This attitude of optimism and "thankfulness in every situation" is surely a prized character attribute, and the one Sarah Palin chose to comment upon regarding her dear husband in a few sentences during this important speech, and the one she states she is going to emulate as her lifetime goes on with him.

But this attitude of willingness to serve her as her "right hand" is the one she mentions first "among his many winning qualities."[33] It reminds me of the one who sits at the right hand of the Father (Ephesians 1:20), who "being in very nature God, did not consider equality with God something to be grasped, but made himself nothing, taking the very nature of a servant, being made in human likeness. And being found in appearance as a man, he humbled himself and became obedient to death – even death on a cross! Therefore God exalted him to the highest place and gave him the name that is above every name, that at the name of Jesus every knee should bow in heaven and on earth and under the earth, and every tongue confess that Jesus Christ is Lord, to the glory of God the Father" (Philippians 2:6-11).

I think only the best of men would assume this role of Christ's, as a servant to all, taking the lowliest position on our behalf. Todd's has been a servant role in many respects, being willing to serve as her advisor and helper in these very critical days that have climaxed just weeks ago. I think one quality of a "real man" I greatly admire is not the measure of his strength or authority, but how he comes under his woman with strong and firm supporting hands and a soft shoulder to cry on, should the more cruel events of life demand one. This is a man who is not threatened by the strongest of her strengths, but because the two of them are "one" in God, seizes the opportunity to help her be the best she can be, and in doing so he becomes the best he can be as a leader.

Not that Todd was any kind of a *mamby-pamby* before Sarah's opportunities for glory came about. Todd, the First Gentleman (the self-styled "First Dude)[34] of Alaska was born September 6, 1964, just about the time his childhood sweetheart would have begun to crawl. He was the spankin' baby boy of James F. "Jim" Palin and his wife Blanch.[35] His father is a former general manager of Matanuska Electrical Association,[36] and is a native of Seattle.[37] His mother was a former secretary of the Alaska Federation of Natives, and she is one quarter Yup'ik. And his mother's mother is a member of the Curyung tribe.[38]

It must have been this strong blood of the Native Americans that gave him some of his strength, endurance and courage for things beyond the physical and emotional guts of many of us. I speak of his record as four-time winner of the Tesoro Iron Dog championship, a snowmobile race which traces the path of the Iditarod (dog sled) race with an extra journey of several hundred miles to Fairbanks added in. He was defending his championship in his most recent race in 2008, yet 400 miles (640 kilometers) from the finish when he was thrown 70 feet from his machine, breaking his arm. He managed to finish the race in fourth place, though he was sent to the hospital with his injuries.[39]

This rugged outdoorsman spirit has also served him well as co-owner and operator of a commercial fishing business, and as a production operator for BP in the North Slope oil fields of Alaska, among other bold adventures I'm sure I have yet to discover.

But young men of the world take note: It's not the strongly physical endeavors he has succeeded in such as the Iron Dog Race that make him so strong. Nor is it the wisdom to run his own company that makes him so wise. It is his willingness and ability to perform well in a nourishing and supportive role in his family that makes him a real hero in my opinion. Ephesians 5:25,29 (NKJV) says, "Husbands, love your wives, just as Christ also loved the Church, and gave Himself for her ... So husbands ought to love their own wives as their own bodies; he who loves his wife loves himself. For no one ever hated his own flesh, but nourishes and cherishes it, just as the Lord does the Church." Jesus Christ is the ultimate loving and selfless leader.

We haven't yet discussed the role of the most famous women who ever existed ... that is the mother of Jesus Christ of Nazareth. She would be the one who so pleased God's heart that she was able to hear the angel one day in her small house proclaim, "Do not be afraid, Mary, you have found favor with God. You will be with child and give birth to a son, and you are to give him the name Jesus, He will be great and will be called the Son of the Most High" (Luke 1:30-32a).

She was the chosen one out of all the young women in Israel at the time, to bring forth the Messiah. She would bear the child who would one day deliver all mankind from our bondage to sin by living the perfect life, dying one of the most painful deaths, and taking the punishment we deserve for our sins by enduring the agony of not only the cross, but the sentence in hell following it. This child conceived by the Holy Spirit within Mary was to be the most important human being to ever walk the face of the earth, and yet even he needed an earthly daddy to be an example and nurture him for this most history-breaking and history-making role in all of eternity. God chose this man, the earthly daddy, Joseph, to take upon himself a unique and protective role, as the man behind the most important woman in history. He was the one who believed in her words of destiny that the angel had spoken to her; he is the one who could bear the possible infamy as one who was thought responsible for the pregnancy of a young woman he had not yet married. He is the one who could protect her, walk the distance with her, and even take her to a foreign land to guard her life and that of the infant boy who had a destiny upon his life.

First and foremost of his admirable characteristics was his ability to hear the voice of God, and his willingness to obey it, trusting Himself and his family into God's hands.

This man Joseph is the hero I would want my boys to emulate; this leader who led by example is one man I highly respect. That's the kind of man I see in Todd Mitchell Palin. I believe he didn't struggle with the destiny he could see God had prepared for the woman who had been his "childhood sweetheart," as she climbed one political rung after another on her way to the race for Vice President of the United States of America, and potentially beyond. I believe he was and is a man with such strength of personality that he can walk alongside a strong woman in multiple ways without being intimidated by her God-given strengths.

I once delivered a Christmas message entitled, "God didn't choose only a woman; He chose a family for the Christ child." I went on to describe some attributes of not only Mary and Joseph, but also Mary's cousin Elizabeth and her husband Zechariah, parents of John the Baptist. John was the one who would have the infamous role of making proclamation in the same spirit as Elijah, (Malachi 4:6) ... preparing the way for the coming one who would bring "repentance and forgiveness of sins to Israel" (Acts 5:31), and also to all mankind throughout human history. God didn't prepare only a woman as a chosen vessel for the Christ child, but a whole family who would take integral parts in His historic destiny. Family matters.

I think perhaps this Todd Palin has had the spiritual insight to see through God's eyes a measure of the destiny upon his wife, and the strength of character to guard and protect her in similar ways that Joseph did for his wife, Mary. He has had the strength to stand behind her and their little family through thick and thin. I'll never forget what a gentle giant of a man Todd seemed to be as he held and cuddled the precious baby Trig, standing firm with each of his other children also as their mom went forward to take her place of destiny on August 29, 2008 in the history of the United States of America. We have no way of knowing what destiny God has in store for the little babies in that picture who could have been legally aborted, never to discover the depths of it. But we do know that God has placed a strong and courageous guard over them, in a similar fashion that He set Joseph of old to guard Mary, the mother of our Christ.

In looking at his work history, we see that Todd had worked for 18 years in the North Slope oil fields of Alaska. But he took a leave from his job as production supervisor, in order to avoid a conflict of interest relating to Sarah's position as governor, as his wife's administration became involved in natural gas pipeline negotiations with Todd's employer. And seven months later to gain more income for the family, he returned to work for BP; this time accepting a non-management position as a production operator, so as to avoid potential conflict of interest. [40]

I believe the Biblical Joseph may have spread his own garments for Mary to lie down and birth the Christ child into the world's history for all eternity. And in a similar fashion Todd has laid down some things so Sarah could walk into her God-given destiny as a strong symbol standing for truth and righteousness, upholding the principles she had learned in the Word of God throughout the years. In doing so she became a heroine not only for myself but for countless women, men and young people in the world today, even the ones many would have thrown away – the many Down Syndrome or other special-needs children Sarah and Todd had the privilege to meet along the campaign trail.

As she and Todd "walked their talk" of faith and dependence upon Jesus and His principles, they have together fulfilled an awesome and weighty destiny in the world, even though she didn't win the seat of Vice President of the United States of America.

In considering the Palin family as she once again takes her seat in the office of the Governor of Alaska, I am intrigued by something said by Gregg Erickson, columnist for the Anchorage Daily News, that Todd Palin "obviously plays an important role ... I've seen him in the governor's office, and I know she's conducted interviews in the governor's office with him present."[41] Palin is occasionally copied on e-mails dealing with official state business. He helped write the state budget, has been involved in personnel matters, and has called lawmakers when he or his wife has disagreed with what they have done. He has advised Governor Palin on workforce development issues as well.[42] These look like some pretty rare opportunities he gets to share with his wife.

These events remind me of the prophetic words of Jesus, recorded for us in Matthew 23:11, "… whoever exalts himself will be humbled, and whoever humbles himself will be exalted."

I believe this principle has been exhibited in Todd Palin, who has exhibited Christ-like behavior in so many special ways with his wife and family, trusting that God will raise him up to such places of greater honor, influence or responsibility as only He can, as He sees fitting and appropriate.

We see Mr. Palin also serving his community over the years as a volunteer, working in youth sports, coaching hockey and basketball.[43] Additionally, he has counseled young people on career choices as they finish high school, encouraging some who can't afford college to consider jobs in the oil and gas industry as an effective training ground.[44]

In summary, I believe Todd Palin gives us a real-life example of one who lives out the principles of being a servant leader, as our Lord Jesus defined above, and seems to reap the benefits and privileges in his marriage and family, his private life, and his professional areas of service and influence. Disney Family Entertainment quotes Sarah Palin with this statement: "Sarah credits her husband Todd as the reason she can govern while raising five kids. 'I am thankful to be married to a man who loves being a dad as much as I love being a mom, so he is my strength.' "[45] Go, First Dude!

CHAPTER FIVE

FAMILY MATTERS

The Palin children are known for their unusual names.[46] Todd is quoted as saying, "Sarah's parents were coaches and the whole family was involved in track and I was an athlete in high school, so with our first-born I was like, 'Track!'

The second child, a girl, 'Bristol' is named after Bristol Bay. That's where I grew up; that's where we commercial fish.

Willow is a community here in Alaska. And then Piper, you know, there are just not too many Pipers out there and it's a cool name."[47] (Also Todd's airplane is a Piper Cub.) "And Trig is a Norse name for "strength.[48]"

As it turns out, each of these precious children is unique, made by God to fulfill a certain sort of destiny in the larger scheme of things. Psalm 139 13-17 says:

> "For you created my inmost being; You knit me together in my mother's womb. I

praise you because I am fearfully and wonderfully made; your works are wonderful, I know that full well. My frame was not hidden from you when I was made in the secret place. When I was woven together in the depths…your eyes saw my unformed body. All the days ordained for me were written in your book before one of them came to be. How precious to me are your thoughts, O God! How vast is the sum of them! Were I to count them, they would outnumber the grains of sand."

Over the years I have found it so comforting to hold these truths of the Scripture close to my heart, trusting in the plans God has for my own children, even as He spoke comforting words to the people of Israel when they were in a "time out" of sorts, "For I know the plans I have for you," declares the Lord, "plans to prosper you and not to harm you, plans to give you a hope and a future" (Jeremiah 29:11). As Christian parents it challenges us to seek God for His guidance in helping to mold the incredibly vulnerable and pliable creations He has put into our care. And as they grow older, it behooves us to also help them seek the Lord for themselves, and for His revelation of their special life purposes and His ways they can come into training and sequential experiences to help them apprehend the fullness of what God has planned for them.

I remember one situation that was life-changing for my daughter. When she was in high school, she had picked up somewhere a flier telling about a traveling group made up of singers and instrumentalists. Their purpose was to travel to various places in the U.S. giving concerts at churches and civic buildings to encourage believers to a deeper walk, and seekers to a point of firm commitment of faith in the Lord Jesus Christ.

We prayerfully decided this was a God-given opportunity to use her skills in playing oboe and English horn for the benefit of the Kingdom of God. Then as for all of us, days and times got busy, and suddenly she and I realized she was right up against the wall of the time to send in her application to participate in this adventure across the Southeastern United States. In looking closely at the application we discovered she needed to send in a tape recording of herself playing her instrument, as well as the required paper work.

As we looked at our watches, it was already mid-evening the night before the application was due in to the ministry leaders. We were tempted to just "give up," leaving it to yet another year ... possibly. Then we prayed, and it did seem that the Lord wanted her to press on with pursuing this opportunity in spite of the obstacles. We found the tape recorder hiding somewhere in the house, and lo and behold the batteries were run down. So as she began to fill out the paper work, I got in the car and ran to the nearest convenience store for more batteries.

It was late in the evening when we got the application all put together, and we decided I would call the next day to see if they would accept a late application. We sent the required materials out the next day, and when I called the ministry leader he explained the unusual circumstances on his end. The oboe player scheduled to go on the tour had come down with some serious illness, and she would not be able to participate. So there was an immediate opening, and they would indeed consider her late application. The rest is history. She spent most of the summer on her first mission trip of sorts, and it changed not only many lives of people who attended the presentations, but the lives of the young people ministering in such a way for the Lord.

I tell this little story to encourage all of us who are parents, grandparents or significant care-givers of young people in our lives. We are responsible to pray for them, to seek God for His revelation of His plans for their lives, and

80

sometimes to "press" with them against challenging circumstances and even powers of darkness to help them apprehend that for which they have been apprehended. Paul said in Philippians 3:12 "...I press on to take hold of that for which Christ Jesus took hold of me."

As for the Palin family, let's examine briefly a few glimpses of each one of their children. I believe we will see that Todd and Sarah have had just this kind of guardianship and godly influence into their children's lives, not only for satisfying life experiences, but for their potential impact in the Kingdom of God.

CHAPTER SIX

TRACK'S TRACKS

He looked so handsome and strong that night, the fateful night of Sarah's acceptance of the party's nomination for vice presidential candidate. He stood tall and true in the uniform of the country he is proud to serve. But how young he looked, and how vulnerable he seemed in light of the serious conflict he would be dropped into only days later, on no other than September 11, 2008, the anniversary of 9/11, a day of horror in the memories of Americans.

Again, God's timing seemed so wonderfully orchestrated. Here for the entire world to see was a bold declaration of dedication when it cost something. And I believe the lives of his father and his mother had gone far to exemplify before him the servant heart that would give up personal goals for larger goals of country, and personal freedoms for the sake of oppressed peoples.

Following is a quote from *People Magazine's Best of 2008;* "Sarah Palin Sees Her Son Off to Iraq."

"Sarah Palin formally sent her nineteen year old son, Track, off to Iraq, with a speech before his unit in Fairbanks, Alaska. 'As you depart us, your parents, your friends and family, if you allow for a few tears and (allow us) to hold you closer before you're gone,' she told the troops of the Army's 1st Stryker Brigade, Delta Company on Thursday…[49]

The Republican vice presidential candidate didn't mention her son by name in her remarks during the deployment ceremony that coincided with the 7th anniversary of the 9/11 terrorist attacks. Members of Track's unit are expected to begin arriving in Iraq over the next few weeks. In an interview with PEOPLE in June, Sarah Palin said she was proud of her son, but that, 'Track didn't ask our permission to sign up.' 'He's young, strong and smart; and this is a good positive step for him,' she added. 'He gave up hockey to do this, and I'm very supportive. I believe in the cause, and hope and pray we have a worthy cause.'[50] Army Col. Burt Thompson, who heads Track's unit at Fort Wainright, Alaska, told the *Anchorage Daily News* that Track receives no preferential treatment. After training in the Mojave Desert this summer, his unit is believed to be headed to Diyala, the 4th most violent of Iraq's provinces. He will operate an armored eight-wheeled, 19 ton vehicle called a Stryker, and serve as a bodyguard for brigade leaders. Track's father, Todd Palin, whose dad is an Army vet, told PEOPLE his only regret was that Track – who has an Alaska tattoo on his shoulder and a Christian fish on his calf – didn't investigate other branches of the service more thoroughly before enlisting. But he supports his son's decision. 'He's looking forward to it,' Todd said. 'He's an independent young man.' " [51]

A week after the election of November 4, Sarah Palin addressed the Republican Governors of America, and said this, "And I'm going to remember all the people along the way who said that they were praying for us; they were such a strength and shield of prayer warriors. Then I remember the Blue Star Moms, and the special bonds we share with our loved ones away at war; I'm going to remember all the veterans of war and the POW's that I had such an honor of meeting and hearing stories … and America can not forget and we must honor and respect these men who have sacrificed so greatly for us and have such a love of country and need to be heard today."[52] Truly her head and heart are tuned into the sacrifices of current and past warriors for our country.

Only history will tell us what Track will give up in the days and years ahead as he fulfills the duty of his heart in the dusty heat and the peal of bullets and explosions in Iraq.

What a picture I hold of this family in my heart: as Sarah goes forth into one destiny, Track goes forth into a destiny of his own ... both into sacrificial service for a country they love and cherish. Let us try to remember to pray for Track as he finds his tracks in the sands of time and history, and let us also remember to ask for the experience described so vividly in the "Footprints" poem, that when there was only one set of footprints in the sand, it did not represent walking alone, but rather being carried in the strong arms of the Savior. May Track's tracks line up with our Lord's, either way.

CHAPTER SEVEN

BRISTOL'S BRAVERY

Who was that young man standing next to her in the audience that fateful day of Sarah Palin's acceptance ceremony for the Republican candidacy for vice president? We are told he is Levi Johnston, the one who hasn't fled from responsibility to the child he has fathered and the woman he loves. But the man who is taking his very real and growing responsibilities (and privileges I might add) very seriously, demonstrating to the entire world his commitment to "stand by my girl" through thick and thin.

The picture could easily have looked very different from the one I saw on television that night. There could have been a blank space where they would have stood, had it not been for the compassion and dedicated love of the parents standing also with them. I think many parents might have excluded them from this family portrait, thinking of the embarrassment it might be for them in such a history-making time of their lives and careers.

But I respect deeply the heart of these parents, who chose to forgive the choices that led to a pregnancy a little out of the optimal sequence of things. And anyway, to be honest, if we were to pass judgment on this young couple, who could stand? For I would guess that a majority of American men and women could truthfully say, "There but for the grace of God go I."

It was a picture of family ties that can go deeper than ever in times like this, and love that forgives, includes and embraces even in the times that could prove to be somewhat embarrassing. What an affirming measure of "worth" in their eyes the Palin parents put upon their oldest daughter, as they encouraged her to be "one of the family" who they were presenting for all the world to see that day. Would that we could all see such ways to help our children experience their worth, not only in our eyes, but in the eyes of their creator God and the communities they find themselves in. I can see all the more clearly one truth in this picture. "Family matters!" Yes, it does.

I can't help wondering what went on in Bristol and Levi's minds and hearts in the days before this monumental day. Did they wonder if they should attend the ceremony, or if they could hold up against the public scrutiny it would involve? But in the end, they did stand up with the rest of the family who stood up with them. The statement to the watching eye was one of a family that loves and forgives and includes ... a family that will cherish life, seeing the God-given blessing in every innocent child in the womb, a person with a destiny of their own yet to unfold.

One could not help but see the clearest picture I can imagine of respect for human life, even the unborn and less-than-perfect from some standards of the world – but in God's eyes perfectly loved just the way he/she is made, with a destiny only He knows the fullness of.

I've seen a number of anti-abortion posters and bill boards in my years of concern for the issue of abortion, but never one so beautiful and full of love and bravery for all concerned. I must tip my hat to an American family that I can truly respect and look up to ... a family that is not above us all in some unreal photograph of perfection. But this is a family I can relate to, who have demonstrated some of the deep qualities God loves best, even in less than ideal circumstances.

There's an old saying, **"Two wrongs don't make a right."**

But there's also a new and better statement, **"Two rights can right a wrong!"**

       Perceived wrongs: 1. Pregnancy out of wedlock

                                        2. Abortion

       Rights: 1. Cherish LIFE! Don't abort a child.

                                        2. Keep the baby and love it with the help of extended family and friends, or bless another family with a beautiful creation.

It is my prayer that many more mothers and fathers facing this decision will make the right choice, and choose to **cherish life**, as Bristol and Levi have.

And as Bristol, blossoming into the beauty of an advancing pregnancy, will have some extra hurdles to overcome along her path, I am confident that "Mom and Dad" will find it a joy and privilege to be with her all the way.

CHAPTER EIGHT

WILLOW'S WISTFUL WAYS

This very attractive fourteen year old brunette has sometimes been mistaken for her older sister, Bristol. And I'm not surprised, as she seems a little precocious in both appearance and behavior. In photos of her with her mom, I can see a striking resemblance between them also. One photo shows Sarah and Willow close together; Sarah was slightly behind her, caressing her shoulder lovingly. They were both looking in the same direction ahead of them, and it almost seemed that together they would see into the future of what it holds for America's young women.

In a section of Sarah's address to the Republican Governors a week after the November 4th presidential election of 2008, she said this of her experience on the campaign trail through America's towns and cities:

"For years to come I'm going to remember all the young girls who came up to me at rallies to see the first woman having the privilege of carrying our party's vice presidential nomination, and they inspired me. With an extra hurdle or two in front of us, in front of these young girls, I feel that we've got this mutually responsible relationship now, these young girls and me, where we're going to work hard; we're going to be stronger; we're going to be better. And one day one of them is going to be president, because in America there will be no ceilings on achievement, class or otherwise. And if I can help point the way for these young women, or inspire them to tap into their own gifts and talents and strengths to find their own opportunities, well it is a privilege."[53]

Willow has been at such in impressionable age during this whirlwind of hotel rooms, rallies, dinners, meetings, handshakes and countless other new experiences, traveling with her mom and dad to some of these cities during this political campaign.

You can't help but wonder what effect it will have on such a strong young woman. I can't help but think that perhaps the resemblance of mother and daughter will be far more than just physical appearance. It's a season of life when young girls tend to focus on a role model – whether it be a recording artist, a movie star, a popular and beautiful

"Hannah Montana" type model or a successful and famous politician such as Sarah Palin. But it wouldn't surprise me a bit if she doesn't set her sights on some of the same goals and aspirations as her mother, the "right in her face" role model. She's still young enough to make some of the choices for courses of study, career or college that could catapult her in the same general direction as her mom. But time will tell, and for now she's just a lovely and sensitive young woman enjoying a very exciting time in her life.

Other photos I've enjoyed reviewing are ones when she is close to or holding baby brother, Trig. Her smile could hardly be broader as she looks on while Cindy McCain (John McCain's lovely wife) is holding Trig and seems to be cooing to him quite admiringly. In another Willow holds him tenderly while baby sister Piper pats him gently on the back.[54]

One private peek into a family conversation is strikingly touching. Sarah and Todd had apparently thought it best not to tell the children that the baby-to-come would have Down Syndrome. On April 18, 2008, she gave birth to 6-lb, 2-oz. Trig, five weeks early. As Todd and their three daughters gathered around the bedside (as Track, an Army private, listened in by phone from his base in Fairbanks) Willow said of the new arrival, "He looks like he has Down Syndrome." Mother Sarah, who says her qualms were laid to rest the minute Trig was born, answered with a lump in her throat. "If he does, you will still love him, Willow. It'll be okay."[55]

Later Willow pressed: "But why didn't you tell us?" Sarah admitted she didn't know how to break the news. "I was a little shocked," says Willow, "but I don't care – he's my brother and I love him." [56]

This remark clicked on a link in my brain to an old print I saw as a child. I think it may have been one by Norman Rockwell or a March of Dimes poster; it seems it may have been on the front of a greeting card as well. It was one of a young man carrying a small boy on his shoulders to some destination unknown. In my memory of it, the boy seemed to be asleep, exhausted from the trek to wherever they were going. Were there crutches in the picture, or is it only my imagination? I'll have to look it up somewhere. Anyway, it seemed they were tramping through the snow in an open field or down a little path. The caption below the print read, "He's not heavy; he's my brother."

One could make a poster shot for siblings of those with Down Syndrome or similar special needs with the same caption. In the Palin family, the weight of this special-needs baby will not be too heavy, and the story of carrying it will bless innumerable thousands of special-needs families throughout America and beyond.

Everything we see or read about Willow seems to demonstrate that she indeed does love Trig dearly. In Sarah's busy life as governor, there will surely by necessity be caregivers who will help her with the responsibilities of caring for the baby. And husband Todd may pick up much of the slack, I would guess. But it seems to be a natural expectation that young Willow will be a primary one to give this child the maternal care he needs on days when mommy is absent. He will not lack for attention and affection.

And this impressionable young woman, while observing both her sister and mother making the right choices to cherish and preserve precious lives, could possibly one day be an incredible advocate for the lives of the unborn or for issues of special-needs children.

One can only surmise at this point, but I'll be watching, knowing that "there are no toilets in God's Kingdom," to quote my husband Dave. By this he means that God is so adept at multi-tasking, He is well able to use every situation for our good as we trust in Him, and allow ourselves to be conformed into the image of Jesus Christ by the experiences we face in life. None of our experiences, nor our tears are wasted in His economy. Looking again at Bible verse Romans 8:28, let's add verses 29 and 30 also: (28) "And we know that in all things God works for the good of those who love Him, who have been called according to His purpose. (29) For those God foreknew, he also predestined to be conformed to the likeness of His Son, that he might be the firstborn among many brothers. (30) And those He predestined He also called; those He called he also justified; those he justified He also glorified."

I remember hearing my mother use a saying that I didn't understand, and I had to ask her to explain the meaning. She said concerning someone who was exceptionally skilled in using some questionable resource, "He could turn a sow's ear into a silk purse." (Maybe she had learned this through her long years of being married to a successful hog farmer!) She further explained that this meant some people have the knack or art of turning even the most undesirable or unattractive things into something beautiful. It was a parable I will never forget, and my eyes tear-up even in the rehearsing of this special memory of my mother, now deceased.

She wasn't talking about God, but she could have been. Much of what I learned about Him came through the many hours of Sunday school classes I had with her as my teacher. What a lucky girl I was! But she could just as well have been talking about God, for He is truly the supreme expert in taking the things we think are mistakes or disadvantages or hindrances to our lives ... and making them into something truly lasting and supremely beautiful, or "glorified", to borrow from verse thirty. I think we're all going to see and hear of some astonishingly beautiful things in the years ahead that God does with and through this family because of baby Trig.

When I think of "willow" I think of and see a tree in mind's eye. This tree is one of the most beautiful of deciduous trees to look at, with its long and swooping branches sometimes reaching to the ground in graceful arches. But it is known not only for its beauty, but also for its flexibility and the strength that comes with flexibility. My prayer is that this already lovely young girl will grow increasingly into a beautiful and creative woman as she develops the flexibility it will require to have a busy governor for a mom, and two active siblings to help look after, one of whom has some special needs. May He give her abounding love and special patience that will enhance her beauty of character and usefulness in His Kingdom.

Then there's to be considered the bird, the Willow Ptarmigan, Alaska's state bird. It is a sedentary species, breeding in birch and other forests in Alaska and Northern Canada. It is a strikingly beautiful bird with a reddish neck and brown upper body, and a white belly. Amazingly, in winter both sexes' plumages become completely white, except that the tail is black. It is also known as the "willow grouse."[57]

One paragraph of its description especially caught my eye: "The male willow grouse is unique in its nesting behavior. In all other species of grouse, only the female takes responsibility for the young. However, the male Willow Grouse often takes responsibility of the young by staunchly defending his territory and his young. Males have been documented to have attacked a grizzly bear and will attack humans who distract their young. The male's call is a loud 'go back go-back.' "[58]

I don't know if Todd and Sarah knew these facts when choosing a name for Willow, but this description seems to fit Willow and also her dad quite well. She seems to have a strong knack for caring for the young ones in the family, and he for defending his family and territory quite effectively, with head alert to bring wise counsel and loud warnings as necessary. And both are very attractive specimens of the human species. The ability of the birds to change their appearance to white in the winter speaks of adaptability for preservation of life against foes of their species in a vulnerable season.

I believe this is a prophetic name given to a very special young woman who may play a major role in the preservation of the young and undefended in America, perhaps both the unborn and those with special needs.

Only time will tell if these predictions will come to pass, but nevertheless our prayer is that she will discern, pursue and embrace God's best plans for her life, whatever they might be.

CHAPTER NINE

PIPER'S PLAY

Play ... that's what life is mostly about for most little girls of seven. Making believe, pretending, trying on roles too big for them; it's a part of little girls with baby dolls, nurse's and doctor's bags, or miniature vacuum cleaners; or little boys with GI Joes, Army trucks or Luke Skywalker figures. Or in this day and age we could reverse the gender on these lists and still be accurate. Someone has said that play is the work of children. How blessed we are in America that our children usually have the opportunity for play. I have recently received pictures of displaced families in refugee camps in India whose homes and sometimes family members were burned by extremists who didn't like their choice of God. They don't seem to have any opportunity for play... no toys and hardly anything to make toys out of; and perhaps no heart for play even if they had them.

Yes, America is still a land of voluminous and varied opportunities; sadly we have so many we don't often appreciate as we should how blessed we are. I don't think little Piper had any real comprehension of what a "big deal" it was to sit in the audience with the members of her family, while mommy went forward to receive one of the highest honors American women have every received. It was just another day, another opportunity for playing pretend.

A very special and endearing memory is the one of little Piper holding her baby brother Trig on her lap during the acceptance ceremony for her mother's V.P. candidacy. I don't know if she was pretending playing "mommy," or just acting out her familiar role as big sister. It doesn't matter; it was a precious memory of a moment to hold onto for a lifetime.

There she was holding little Trig on her lap, stroking him gently in what seemed to be a familiar adoring and calming routine. Then I saw a most endearing sight that caused me to stare in wonderment. Piper licked the palm of her little hand, and then ran it over the top of baby Trig's head to smooth down some errant strands of hair, so he would be at his best for this momentous occasion. But once didn't seem to do the trick – she repeated the hair spit-polishing maneuver several times until she was satisfied that he was presentable enough for this important moment.

Little did she know that he was actually the "king" of the tabloid this family represented that day. And big sister Bristol was the "queen." They were the monarchs representing the high standard of conduct exemplified by our Lord Jesus Christ, and recorded for generations unto all eternity to consume and be consumed by. For the Bible says that His Word will last forever. They were the living proof texts on display for the entire world to see, unashamedly living out the real life results of hard decisions made according to the confines of the true Word of God … and not the convenience and comforts of selfish people who are looking for a quick fix. The moments of this screen play almost took away my breath; I was so captivated by what I was seeing – for coming out for display before my very eyes were the heroes and heroines I had waited 60 years for. I thought, "Maybe it's not quite too late for America!"

I couldn't help wondering if Piper had thought of this hair management technique all by herself, or had she seen it demonstrated by someone bigger and wiser that herself? No matter – it was a real show-stealer, and I'm amazed the camera got back to the event at hand in time to catch the action of Sarah Palin's acceptance speech. Someday when Trig is bigger, he'll enjoy seeing this video, the solid and

107

perhaps comical evidence of how much his little big sister loved and cared for him, even as a small baby. Trig will experience the joys of life! Hallelujah!

Another show-stopping piece of video I saw recently was Piper carrying Trig around the kitchen while mom and dad prepared a special fish recipe. Simultaneously an interviewer from the Today Show asked hard grown-up questions.[59] And all this time she was wearing play high-heeled shoes! A highly charged moment for her parents was just another opportunity for pretend play for precious Piper.

Other very interesting photos have shown Piper wearing glasses just like Mom's, black boots just like Mom's, blouses the same style and color as Mom's, and yes – she ever waves at the crowd like Mom does. [60]

These photos said volumes about where Piper is right now in her development. Just big enough to idolize her mom, dress like her, wave like her, and who knows what else that's not open for general public consumption – like her. It's a poignant reminder for us as parents, grandparents, older siblings and extended family members, that the little ones in our care or our environment are watching everything we do, and hearing everything we say. They are impressionable, malleable little learners, for better or for worse. I do believe that most of the examples Piper sees at home are for the good, thanks to the influence of a righteous God and an instruction manual with specific weighty directions such as: "Imitate me just as I also imitate Christ" (1 Corinthians 11:1, NKJV), and "Fathers, do not provoke your children, lest they become discouraged" (Colossians 3:21 NKJV), and also "Train up a child in the way he should go…" (Proverbs 22:6).

Back to my photo gallery for one last look, there was a "show-stopper" of Sarah and Piper on what looked like a stage. Both were dressed in gray and black outfits. Sarah was several steps ahead of Piper, and following in her footsteps was Piper, taking her steps with the same foot first and similar hand motions. They looked almost like a Vaudeville act; but it was not an act. She was doing what happens to come naturally – imitating her mom, and having a good time at it. [60]

Wandering through this photo gallery gave me a lot of inspiration, but also a painful reminder of some times when my children were watching me, and I gave them behaviors to imitate that weren't at all edifying to imitate. Oh that I could do it again differently; but I can't. The words are already spent and hopefully most have fallen from little memories along the ways and years of my children's lives.

I'm not good at reading instruction manuals, and Dave sometimes pokes fun at me when I hand the hard "how to put it together" projects over to him. But I've discovered that there's one life-building manual that serves me better and better the more times I read it. God's Word, the Bible, is true and endures forever. His Word really is "living and active. Sharper than any double-edged sword, it penetrates even to dividing soul and spirit, joints and marrow; it judges the thoughts and attitudes of the heart" (Hebrews 4:12). And it changes us over the course of time for the better; there is always hope with the Master Builder.

I remember the story of the Pied Piper from some story or poem book long ago lost from my possession. As I remember it, he went through the streets of town playing his pipe, and others followed him around until there was a large crowd.

Our prayer for this little family is that mom and dad and older siblings can continue by God's grace to pipe a tune in the behavior of their day-to-day lives that little Piper (Trig too) can mimic in their play and in the serious moments of their lives as they grow up – a tune of righteousness and holy living that girls and boys and men and women in the years to come can follow, bringing a smile to their parent's faces and also to God's. These two are also learning lessons to **cherish life.** God bless you Piper.

CHAPTER TEN

TRIG'S TRIGGERS

We know that dad and mom are good with triggers, as wild game pictures and trophies have graced their walls from various hunting expeditions over the years. But what we are coming to see right now is that baby Trig is pretty adept at triggers himself. Born in April of the year of this book, 2008, we see this little life triggering responses from people all over the world. His very being, the very breaths he breathes and pictures of life he demonstrates evoke the release of triggers in the lives of an on-looking world.

For some it triggers judgments such as, "Why did they make the decision not to abort this child? He can never fill a useful place in society!" Or for others his life will trigger rejoicing in what is true and right in God's eyes according to 1 Corinthians 13:6 "Love does not delight in evil but rejoices with the truth." God's eternal Truth says, "You shall not murder" (Exodus 20:13). As I find these verses in my NIV and Dave's NKJV and Mother's Living Bible, the word "murder" somehow seems stronger than the "kill" in "Thou shall not kill" of previous versions of the Bible. Murder seems so heinous and foul, so premeditated and purposefully evil. It's different than the "kill" I accidentally did to the unfortunate little porcupine who wandered into the road in front of my mini-van a few weeks ago after dark.

No, murder seems planned, having made a choice to purposefully take a life. I think many young and unfortunate victims of the abortion abomination, are the girls and women who are lied to and tricked into believing that the unborn baby is not really a "life" and so it's OK to take it away. Such a sad and tragic day it is for them when they discover it was really a life, and now it is gone. Such a foul thing is the gift certificate that is for sale this Christmas season for services at Planned Parenthood. It can be purchased and given to the woman of your choice. Granted it could be used towards a well-woman exam or treatment of women's ailments, but it could also be applied to the price of an abortion. A nun spoke up on the TV news last evening in strong opposition to the practice which seems to violate the very purpose of Christmas – the celebration of the presentation of life … the greatest life ever lived.

Thank God that He extends love, mercy and forgiveness for even this sin of taking life – abortion – if there is true sorrow and repentance. I praise God for the heroic men and women who fight for LIFE, displaying vividly in color the pictures of little babies at 10 and 12 and 16 weeks of life, still too tiny to make their mommies' tummies bulge much, but with beating hearts and distinct fingers and toes. Taking the lives of these precious little people really is premeditated murder, and blatantly defies God's clear command to us, "You shall not murder."

I praise God that little Trig is alive to breathe and smile and one day run and play, bringing joy to the hearts of his family and onlookers everywhere. This morning in our Bible study and prayer time I sang a line with my husband from a contemporary worship song, "I breathe in the breath that You gave me to breathe, to worship You, to worship You." Yes, Trig's very breath and life evoke worship of the Author of Life, just as he is. He will bring more joy and accomplish greater things in his life than we could ever imagine now.

The *Kids Health* website has a wonderful summary of Down Syndrome and gives credit to Dr. John Langdon Haydon Down, in an English hospital as discovering in 1866 characteristic physical and mental traits common to a certain

115

group of people. Thus the syndrome bears his name. But it was not until almost a century later that a French scientist identified the problem as genetic. *Kids Health* remarks, "But despite their challenges, kids with Down syndrome can go to regular schools, make friends, enjoy life, and get jobs when they're older."[61]

That says a lot! And the site is a wonderful kid-friendly source of general information on a subject most of us, kids and adults alike, need to know more about.

I can't help but remember the words of Psalm 139:13-15, "For you created my inmost being; you knit me together in my mother's womb. I praise you because I am fearfully and wonderfully made; your works are wonderful, I know that full well. My frame was not hidden from you when I was made in the secret place."

I believe little Trig was made by design ... not by accident. He will do more valiant works just as he is than he could have, had he been made with the normal number of chromosomes. Yes, it will be a delight to see just what awesome and monumental things he does in the hearts and lives of Americans and citizens of the world. He was made for just such a time as this. Praise God.

The speech Sarah Palin made before the meeting of Republican Governors a week after the November, '08 election is such a wonderful summary of so many of her life experiences and value statements. Here is a little glimpse of some things she enjoyed and came to treasure along the campaign trail:

"... I will remember with gratitude all the families with special needs children who were the star of the show in our rallies – kids with autism and some in their wheel chairs, and these beautiful kids who maybe before were made to feel that there wasn't a place for them in the life of our country. How could I ever forget the banners that were held up high that say, 'We're here for Trig ... Trig in the White House.' Oh these beautiful children and their families! And I'm always being warned, 'Oh you can't cry on the campaign trail; you can't shed a tear.' Oh My goodness! Speaking to some of these families and the challenges that they have; and they weren't asking anything from government or anyone else – perhaps a hand up but not a hand out. These families I would see in the audience, and they would hold up their banners. And I'll tell you I came close to crying a few times because they just touched my heart. And it's time America showed them our good collective heart.

One of my favorite persons I met along the trail was one of your constituents at a rally right here in Florida, and his name is Charlie; he's a fine young man with Down Syndrome. He's just so proud and strong and tough. And Charlie and I exchanged e-mail addresses. And the last time he replied he said, 'By the way, please quit calling me Darlin.' I was talking about him on the trail once in awhile. And he said, 'It's not *tough* enough.' And so today in your home state, a special <u>shout out</u> to Charlie, to

TOUGH CHUCK ... DARLIN' CHARLIE !!!

And I'll repeat what I told him, because it applies to all children and adults who are so unique:

…. 'that he is beautiful, and I'm so glad that my boy Trig is going to grow to be just like him!'

And every innocent life being so precious and worthy; truly we must show them the good heart of America ... It reminded me of a bumper sticker that was sent to me from a Down Syndrome group in Arizona. You know how we have bumper stickers on our mini-vans across the nation saying … 'My kid's on the honor roll and yours isn't,' etc., and 'My kid's a better soccer player than your kid' (and whatever it is they say). The bumper sticker that was sent to me was, 'My kid's got more chromosomes than your kid!' And I say, 'Alright!

We won; WE WON!'

But I'm so thankful that they (Down Syndrome and special needs kids and families) knew that they were welcome, and that too is what we represent as Republicans ... that good heart of America, that equal opportunity for all and defense of those who are vulnerable and weak. Heaven help us if we ever stray from that principle or from that value in our party. It was wonderful, and I was honored to get to represent that value." [62]

One statement publicized following Trig's birth on April 18, 2008 reads like this:

"Trig is beautiful and already adored by us. We knew through early testing he would face special challenges, and we feel privileged that God would entrust us with this gift and allow us unspeakable joy as he entered our lives. We have faith that every baby is created for a good purpose and has potential to make this world a better place. We are truly blessed!"[63]

Soon after Trig was born, Sarah Palin sent a personal email to close friends and family explaining that their new baby had Down Syndrome. It seems to me the note may have been written as if from God's perspective. It said, "Many people will express sympathy, but you don't want or need that, because Trig will be a joy. Children are the most precious and promising ingredient in this mixed-up world you live in down there on Earth. Trig is no different, except he has one extra chromosome."[64]

From my editorial perspective, that pretty much says it all!

But in all fairness, I need to give Todd and Sarah Palin a chance to have the last word on their new son Trig.

When Todd and Sarah Palin took their baby to the front of the fellowship of the Church to dedicate him to God, they said,

"This little boy is our pro-life statement."[65]

And someday Trig, when you're old enough to read this book, you'll see it is dedicated to you ... **because you're my hero too! "We won, Trig!**

WE WON!"

CHAPTER ELEVEN

GREAT REWARDS

A lot like the "You've Got Mail" sign that keeps popping up on the computer while you're working on something else, I keep getting the "Your God Mail" reminder coming on in my brain. A part of a verse has kept coming up to the surface of my consciousness, and I've ignored it for awhile. But it seems to not let me go on with my other work anymore.

This is what it says, "...in keeping them there is great reward." It looks like a recovered fragment, which is what a lot of my emails from God look like. He takes a fragment that I know and uses it to flag me into a sentence or chapter of the Bible that He wants to remind me of or teach me. It's like a game almost ... that wonderful, exciting, fun and ever unique experience of fellowship with Jesus Christ, the one true Master of the Universe. It seems almost inconceivable sometimes that He would want to have a relationship, or more than that even ... intimate fellowship with little ol' ordinary me. But indeed He does! How awesome is that!

The other day I was in our local computer tech and repair shop, trying to work out some glitches in my laptop, and the technician made casual conversation as he worked on my computer in the same room. It was the first day I had met this young man of 25, but he surprised me by inviting me into his private life, sharing with me a dream he had the night before. He wanted to understand it, and I mentioned that God can interpret dreams, and briefly sketched a bit of Daniel chapter two. I took time to pray inconspicuously, and we discussed possible meanings of his dream. Later in our conversation, he mentioned his own earlier relationship with God, going to church and youth group maybe ten years ago. But, like so many youth, this had lost its meaning for him and he drifted away. He mentioned that he had felt guilty asking so many things of God, and finally just kind of quit talking to God.

This was my "shoe in" to a deeper conversation. In a few words, I tried to relay the message that the "asking" is a lot of what our fellowship with God is all about. He wants us to need Him, to communicate with Him, to ask things of Him, expecting answers back. It's called "fellowship" with God. Just like we parents can get an "empty nest syndrome" when our kids leave home for college or careers, we feel lost and unneeded when our kids aren't communicating with us … a communication that often involves asking something of us.

I tried to help him see that fellowship with God is a lot like that. Though He wants our thanks and praise for the many good things He does for us and gives us, just as we parents like these verbal expressions of appreciation from our kids; the "asking" for things we need – material things, opinions, advice, information, wisdom, etc. is often a huge part of our fellowship with God. And His very great desire is for "fellowship" with each one of us; He created us for just exactly that!

Acts 17:26 says that God determines the times set for us and the exact places where we will live. And verses 27-28 read, "God did this so that men would seek Him and perhaps reach out for Him and find Him, though he is not far from each one of us. For in him we live and move and have our being."

I had more conversation with the man examining my computer, and my intent was to draw him back into the fellowship with God he once had, because it seemed that's what he was fishing for in opening conversation with me. (It had been clear from looking at the names of files in my laptop that I was a minister or something.) Hopefully something sparked an interest longtime dormant, and I'll keep praying for him that he might know true fellowship with God.

I went on my way rejoicing in the interchange that seemed to bring some meaning to the 2.5 hour interruption in my already packed day, accepting and even thanking Jesus for the small crash of my laptop computer that led up to it. For after all, He is Lord, and I am His subject. That's a major clause in the contract we made together in the Christmas season of 1972.

So in my own fellowship with God, I've become accustomed to ways He gets my attention so we can have some deeper fellowship times together. This little fragment of a verse that He brought up several times in the last few days on the exquisite computer of my brain is just one of them.

And it seemed He wasn't going to let me out of this book until I read it. So I considered again the fragment "in keeping them there is great reward" and went on the trail to look up the word "reward" in the concordance in the back of my Bible, and soon found the passage in Psalm 19:9-11: "The ordinances of the Lord are sure and altogether righteous. They are more precious than gold, than much pure gold; they are sweeter than honey, than honey from the comb. By them is your servant warned; **in keeping them there is great reward."**

For several days I've been pondering and praying about what this verse means, and why the Lord had flagged it at this specific time. I came to see that there needs to be an aspect of "balance" brought into our conversation about "cherishing life." I've said some things about "You shall not…." but not so much about the rewards you get when you obey the rules God has given us for our own good.

It seems that obedience and rewards are instilled into our beings at a very early age. If we eat most of our nutritious meal we can have dessert. If we do a good job with our lessons we get a good grade. When we show up to work on time and do our job well, we get paid and are allowed to keep working wherever we work. We may even get a bonus. And the list could go on and on.

Rewards for appropriate behavior are a part of life, and this passage reminds us that God too has rewards for us, ones we can experience when we follow and obey His ordinances, the different words of information and instruction given to us in the Bible. And oh what an awesome and thrilling life quest it is to search them out, learn to obey them ... and also experience the rewards inherit within the process.

We serve an awesome, loving and GOOD God, who wants the best for us, and has given us His Word to help us see how to find it. In my personal quest, it has become my goal to say of my life as Job did, "I have treasured the words of His mouth more than my daily bread" (Job 23:12). I don't feel well physically when I leave home without breakfast; and I don't feel well spiritually when I leave home without my daily time with God. So I don't skip either. It's as simple as that. When I give God the first minutes of my waking day, I experience more of His presence in the remaining hours. Would that I had learned this vital secret years earlier than I did!

In regards to "cherishing life," I am reminded that there are so many ways to cherish life. As my husband and I discussed some of them, we were really surprised at how many we discovered. We thought of ways such as learning to appreciate more the days we have to live on this earth, and we pondered how we might change things if we knew our days were seriously numbered by a terminal illness. We discussed how matters of relationship and fellowship with family members and friends might take a front seat to some material things that we as humans tend to give too much importance sometimes. We pondered how we might make an effort to cherish each other more in our day-to-day life and communication with each other.

Any even more importantly, what are some ways we can cherish life by using our moments and hours and days in ways that line up with the Lord's eternal purposes for our lives, as Paul said, "Not that I have already obtained all this, or have already been made perfect, but I press on to take hold of that for which Christ Jesus took hold of me ... I do not consider myself yet to have taken hold of it. But one thing I do: Forgetting what is behind and straining toward what is ahead, I press on toward the goal to win the prize for which God has called me heavenward in Christ Jesus" (Philippians 3:12-14). This seemed to bring things into focus for me – searching to discover more of the purposes God has ordained for my life and pressing on to take hold of them, expecting that He has rewards for me within them.

When I consider what the rewards may be that I personally seek in my life, I am reminded of the words of Romans 14:17: "For the Kingdom of God is not a matter of eating and drinking, but of righteousness, peace and joy in the Holy Spirit..." That said, for me its not the things that pass away such as meat and drink that I consider to be rewards; instead it is those eternal things, those inner attributes and conditions that I so desire and long for: righteousness, peace and joy in my God through the Holy Spirit. And these things God promises to each and every one of us as an expression of His Kingdom reign and rule in our lives, when we obey His ordinances and the ways of His Kingdom.

The pursuit and discovery of these attributes are a quest worthy of spending our time searching out. I believe there are hidden rewards inherent within the great price expended by many in caring for "special-needs" children. Sarah Palin was told of Trig, "He will be a joy!" And I remember reading and hearing that Down Syndrome children are just that; often not displaying some of the annoying resistance to our direction, or obstinate phases many or most children go through in growing up. And that they experience great pleasure and joy in the discovery of many of the things life has to offer that other children might take for granted. That would surely be a good example to us.

In 2 Peter 1:3-4 we read, "His divine power has given us everything we need for life and godliness through our knowledge of Him who called us by His own glory and goodness. Through these He has given us His very great and precious promises, so that through them you may participate in the divine nature and escape the corruption in the world caused by evil desires." We see that through God's power and his precious promises, He makes provision for us that we might become more like Him. This may prove to be the best goal that we could ever aspire to … and the greatest reward.

We can choose to **cherish life** in a number of different ways in our individual lives. We have discussed a number of them, and I'm sure you have thought of many more. To discuss them all would take another book in itself.

I remember what Jesus said of Himself in John 10:9-10, "I am the gate; whoever enters through me will be saved. He will come in and go out, and find pasture. The thief comes only to steal and kill and destroy; I have come that they may have life, and have if to the full (more abundantly NKJV)." This "abundant life" is what Jesus desires for us, and sometimes it comes in packages we didn't anticipate or expect. We have considered briefly some aspects of the awesome and timely purposes and destiny in the lives of Sarah and Todd Palin and their precious family in this moment of history. And time will reveal how truly immense they have been and will continue to be in the days ahead.

I found for my life a heroine I didn't even know I was searching for. But along with her I discovered a family who are an incredibly visible example to American families and even citizens of the world. And also one I believe we as Christian families can use as role models in many powerful ways. They are not perfect, as none of us are; but neither were Mary and Joseph or the other Biblical characters we have considered and continue to learn from or seek to emulate. We need to learn to walk with God seeking His best for our lives, attempting to right wrongs and **CHERISH LIFE** in the various ways the Lord Jesus might present before us by the Holy Spirit.

APPENDIX

A week following the November 4, 2008 national elections, where Governor Sarah Palin of Alaska ran for Vice President of the United States on the Presidential ticket of Senator John McCain, she was back at her post as Governor of Alaska. In this role, she was a major speaker at the RGA, Republican Governors of America meeting in Florida. This speech was an incredibly crafted summary of many of her recent experiences on the campaign trail; and a highly candid look into the state of the states and union, and future challenges awaiting her and the other Republican governors.

Portions of this speech have been cited in several chapters of this book, but the entire speech contains valuable insights into other aspects of her campaign, her strong statement of personal values, and her goals for the Republican Party, her state and the future of America. This speech summarizes some major aspects of her political agenda that have not yet been covered in this book.

Therefore the speech, almost in its entirety, is included to help you fill in some gaps in her personal values, views, goals, and sound political aspirations for her state and her nation. The text that follows is taken from a transcription of the oral text, begun a short distance into the speech. I apologize for any unintentional omissions or errors; and please understand that the sentence breaks, punctuation, emphasized words and other editorial judgments are purely the best efforts of the editor. Several words or short phrases were omitted due to inability to hear clearly what was spoken. The recovered text follows from the:

Speech Delivered by Sarah Palin, Governor of Alaska, U.S.A., to the assembly of the Republican Governors of America, November 11, 2008.

… We (Alaskans) do things like putting our state checkbook on line so that everybody can see where every dollar is being spent with other people's money. Federal government, we need to do the same thing. We need to be able to help our federal officials see what we do as governors that has led to reform within our state and progress within our state……

Looking back on the campaign, it was such a journey for my family; it was wonderful! But what a nice return it has been to return to a place and a life that we so dearly love in Alaska.

Along the trail it was my husband, Todd who was my right hand, and among his many winning qualities is the gift that he has of optimism and just thankfulness in all situations that he finds. Going forward, I'm going to count on those qualities a little more, even because of course there was a disappointment after a loss of a national election like that. You run the race to win! I was kind of relying on Todd with that optimism of Todd, and the thankfulness in all situations, and I'm certainly going to be there with him along those lines.

But far from returning to the great state of Alaska with any sense of sorrow or regret, we carried with us the best of memories and joyful experiences that really do not depend at all on political victory.

For years to come I'm going to remember all the young girls who came up to me at rallies to see the first woman having the privilege of carrying our party's vice presidential nomination, and they inspired me with an extra hurdle or two in front of us, in front of these young girls. I feel that we've got this mutually responsible relationship now, these young girls and me, where we're going to work harder; we're going to be stronger, we're going to be better; and one day one of them is going to be President, because in America there will be no ceilings on achievement, class or otherwise. And if I can help point the way for these young women, or inspire them to tap into their own gifts and talents and strengths to find their own opportunities, well it is a privilege!

And I'm going to remember all the people along the way who said that they were praying for us; they were such a strength and shield of prayer warriors.

Then I remember the Blue Star Moms, and the special bonds we share with our loved ones away at war. I'm going to remember all the Veterans of War and the POW's that I had such an honor of meeting and hearing their stories…and America can not forget. We must honor and respect these (ones) who have sacrificed so greatly for us, and have such a love of country and need to be heard today.

I'll remember the working people of this country who put their faith in us; the folks who run our factories and grow our food, and teach our children, and serve us in uniform … those who came out on the campaign trail also to say that they had a lot of hope for the ideals that we were representing in our ticket. And I remember folks like "Joe the plumber" who spoke for so many. When "Joe the plumber" remembers and suggested that taking more of our families' and our small businesses' hard earned money, what that does is stifle the entrepreneurial spirit that grew this country into the greatest country on earth. And thanks to "Joe the plumber," people who knew this thing before felt kind of comforted like, "See, I'm not the only one who sees that." ... I'll not forget guys like "Tito the builder." He recently became a U.S. citizen, running his own construction company now.

He, on the trail, was telling us so proudly, "yeah, I was born in Columbia, but I was MADE IN THE USA!" This is the land of opportunity. And to see everyday hard working Americans whom we would meet...and again such a comfort that we had knowing that we're not the only ones believing in America being the land of possibilities and opportunity.

But federal government has to play its appropriate role, not to get in the way of the progress of our families and our businesses ...and for their example and their love too. I will remember with gratitude all the families with special-needs children who were the star of the show in our rallies ... kids with autism and some in their wheel chairs, and these beautiful kids who maybe before were made to feel that there wasn't a place for them in the life of our country. How could I ever forget the banners that were held up high that say, "We're here for Trig ... Trig in the White House!"... and these beautiful children and their families. And I've always been warned, "Oh you can't cry on the campaign trail; you can't shed a tear." Oh my goodness! Speaking to some of these families and the challenges that they have ... and they weren't asking anything from government or anyone else; perhaps a hand up but not a hand-out. These families I would see in the audience, and they would hold up their banners. And I'll tell you I came close to crying a few times, because they just touched my heart; and it's time America showed them our good collective heart.

One of my favorite persons I met along the trail was one of your constituents at a rally right here in Florida, and his name is Charlie. He's a fine young man with Down Syndrome. He's just so proud and strong and tough, and Charlie and I exchanged email addresses. And the last time he replied he said, "By the way, please quit calling me Darlin'." I was talking about him on the trail once in awhile. And he said, "It's not TOUGH enough." And so today in your home state a special shout out to Charlie, to

"TOUGH CHUCK ... Darlin' Charlie!!!"

And I'll repeat what I told him because it applies to all children and adults who are so unique… "that he is beautiful, and I'm so glad that…

my boy Trig is going to grow to be just like him!"

And every innocent life being so precious and worthy, and truly we must show them the good heart of America.

Another funny thing too on the trail, we had a beautiful group of Down Syndrome young adults and children, and they're holding up their signs, and with Down Syndrome of course you're born with an extra chromosome … And it reminded me of a bumper sticker that was sent to me from a Down Syndrome group in Arizona. You know how we have bumper stickers on our mini-vans across the nation saying, you know, "My kid's on the honor roll and yours isn't"… and "My kid's a better soccer player than your kid" (and whatever it is they say). The bumper sticker that was sent to me was, "My kid's got more chromosomes than your kid."

"Alright! We won; <u>WE WON!!</u>"

But I'm so thankful that they knew that they were welcome, and that too is what we represent as Republicans … is that good heart of America, that equal opportunity for all and defense of those who are vulnerable and weak.

Heaven help us if we ever stray from that principle, from that value in our party, and it was wonderful, and I was honored to get to represent that value!

Above all too I am grateful to the man who took a chance on a Republican governor, representing you, representing all of you, and what we believe in and with sound executive experience, and on the front lines every day. That is who you are; that is who we are, making tough decision to best serve the people who hire us, and we are held accountable every day. The buck stops on our desk; we're not just one of many voting "yea" or "nay" or "present." No there is no "present button" in our office, is there? We have to make the tough decisions. John McCain knew what it is that we represent, what I represent and all of you ... from the moment he knew me. On election day I had the rare enough privilege in politics of praising the candidate whose story and character and personal heroism required no embellishment. I said things about him, about how valiantly he has served, and what he has overcome ... things he could not say about himself because that's just the kind of man that he is ... so humble. And elections, granted they're not a test of (acting) valiantly or merit alone of course. And the judgment of the majority is not for us to question now. Enough to say that for me it was the honor of a lifetime to fight for what we believe in at the side of John S. McCain.

So now with the recent elections wrapped up on the federal level, we are now the minority party, but:

Let us resolve not to become the negative party, too eager to find faults, or unwilling to help in a time of crisis and war.

***Losing the election does not have to mean losing our way*!**

And for governors the way forward leads to our own state capitols, in reforms that we will carry on or begin anew.

And I promise you, Americans will be looking to their governors for reaction, for stepped-up leadership, and for our abilities to unite and to progress. Let the pundits go on with their idle talk about the next election and what happens in 2012. Our concern should be about our state's next great reform, our next budget, our next opportunity to progress in the states that we serve; and on issues like taxes and energy and health care, immigration and education. We will not lack for opportunities to serve and to lead and to show the way.

If the new congress and president err on the side, for instance, of excess taxes, then it will be falling on us to show them a better way ... we governors have one of the greatest powers there is in a democracy, and that is a power of example. And we in the RGA must use that power to create the growth and the opportunities and the jobs that come from lower taxes and more efficient bureaucracy for everyone.

Now some things we need to keep our eye on: if I remember correctly from the campaign, the new president and the congressional majority; they have their own ideas about energy policy. I didn't hear a lot from them about *actual* production of U.S. energy supplies that we need now to protect our economy and our nation from reliance on foreign cartels and dictators – those who use energy as a weapon. Maybe though, the fact of having the final responsibility for energy policy will change their outlook. But if not, and again it will be left for the states, for us to point the way. And from the North slope oil fields of Alaska, to the outer continental shelf of Florida, we will press on with the great work of achieving energy security. And we CAN do this; we HAVE to do this. We have the American energy sources, conventional and alternative. We can bring it about by American ingenuity, and we're going to produce it by American workers. And we can do this. Yes!

Other issues that we work on every day in our jobs in public service, when it comes to, for instance, health care;

the goal of affordable, accessible care is a goal that we all share. But there still are serious differences about how we reach this ... while Congress and some of the other Democratic leaders ... and the new President ... while they all debate it, we in the state can still advance our reforms to expand choices and increase competition. And I'm not going to assume that the answer is for the federal government to just take it over and try to run America's health care system. Heaven forbid! Governors, let's lead on this reform front too, with medical savings accounts, and transparency, and medical record keeping, and (reducing) barriers to more choices. Let's just get it done and again show the federal government the way.

And now finally in every great reform effort, there is an element of self reform. And Republicans can not shy away from that challenge either. We must see reform within. The cost of war security cannot explain a federal debt that has grown to more than ten trillion dollars. Washington D.C. leaders spent public money in disregard of the public interest, just like the opponents that they used to criticize. They got too comfortable in power. Maybe they forgot why they were sent to Washington and who they were sent to serve. We're looking now at an American people having to work for their government, instead of our government working for the people, and enough ... enough of that.

All of this must change if we are to lead again in Washington and change Washington for the better. So in the months ahead, let us build our case with actions, and not with just words. And let us reclaim our good name as a party: of spending restraint, and limited government, and economic opportunity, and personal freedom and responsibility and American traditions. Let us be true to our beliefs, strong in the defense of the weak, unafraid to speak for American ideals, and firm in our support for the men and women who defend those ideals in a dangerous world. And in all that that we do, let us carry ourselves with good will and confidence and with a servant's heart. Let us lead by example.

A week ago America did make her choice; and as for us, with a strong group of leaders here – our convictions, our loyalties, our hopes for this country remain the same I am sure. In respect to our presidential campaign, now it is time for us to go our way, being neither bitter nor vanquished, but instead confident in the knowledge that there will be another day, and we will gather once more with new strength and we will rise to fight again.

In the meantime governors, I know, RGA, we're going to be walking the walk of true reform within our own states.

We will lead by example. The nation needs us, and I say, God bless you in your states!

And thank you for all that you are doing for this great country. And we're going to step it up even more so RGA. Thank you guys!

God bless ya'!

REFERENCES

1 *Wikipedia*, Sarah Palin

2 www.hoopsfantasy.com/sarah-palin-basketball-sarah-barracuda/

3 *Wikipedia*, Sarah Palin

4 Ibid.

5 Ibid.

6 *The New York Times*, "Times People, Sarah Palin" November 20, 2008

7 *Wikipedia*, Sarah Palin

8 Web (link.brightcove.com/services/player/bcpid76663834)

9 *Wikipedia*, Sarah Palin

10 *The New York Times*, "Times People, Sarah Palin," November 20, 2008

11 Ibid.

12 Ibid.

13 *Wikipedia*, Sarah Palin

14 Ibid.

15 Ibid.

16 *New York Times*, "Milestones, Sarah Palin," Nov. 29,08

17 Ibid.

18 *Wikipedia*, Sarah Palin

19 *New York Times*, "Milestones, Sarah Palin," Nov.29,08

20 *Wikipedia*

21 *State of Alaska, News & Announcements*, AGIA Passes, Palin Thanks Legislators, August, 2008.

22 *Wikipedia*, Sarah Palin

23 Ibid.

24 Ibid.

25 Ibid.

26 *New York Times*, "Milestones, Sarah Palin," Nov.29,08

27 *Wikipedia*, Sarah Palin

28 Republican Governors of America caucus, Florida, Nov.11, '08, Sarah Palin Address

29 Ibid.

30 Ibid.

31 Ibid.

32 Ibid.

33 Ibid.

34 *Wikipedia*, Todd Palin

35 Ibid.

36 Ibid.

37 Ibid

38 Ibid.

39 Ibid.

40 Ibid.

41 Ibid.

42 Ibid.

43 Ibid.

44 Ibid.

45 *Disney Family Entertainment*, Election Moms: Sarah Palin 2008

46 Ibid.

47 Ibid.

48 Ibid.

49 *People Magazine*, Best of 2008, "Sarah Palin Sees Her Son Off to Iraq."

50 Ibid.

51 Ibid.

52 RGA caucus, Florida, Nov. 2008, Sarah Palin Address.

53 Ibid.

54 *Huffington Post*, Willow Palin Photos: Pictures and Stories of Sarah Palin's Middle Daughter.

55 Ibid.

56 Ibid.

57 *Wikipedia*, Willow Ptarmigan

58 Ibid.

59 *Huffington Post*, November 11, 2008, Piper Palin

60 *Huffington Post*, "Piper Palin 'Sarah' Style," October 29, 2008, Willow Lindley/Anya Strzemien

61 *KidsHealth*, Down Syndrome

62 RGA Caucus, Florida, Nov. 2008, Sarah Palin Address

63 *Huffington Post*, August 29, 2008

64 *Disney Family Entertainment*, "Election Moms: Sarah Palin" Nov., '08.

65 From Repeatedly Forwarded Prayer Request for Sarah Palin Family.

ABOUT THE AUTHOR

Janice Woodrum received Jesus Christ as Lord and Savior in 1972, and experienced a revival and rededication to a deeper walk with the Lord in 1987. She went forward to the altar of a Sutera Brothers crusade in Tacoma, Washington in January of 1991, laying down her life for full time service to the Lord Jesus at whatever time He would see fit to make that possible,

In His infinite wisdom, He chose to open up new avenues of ministry within her church body and community first, and beyond to the foreign field in the Philippines in 1994. Doors for Janice and her husband, Dave, have continued to open as their international mission organization, Harvest of Jubilee Groups, International has spread out into fields including Vietnam, Cambodia, India, Pakistan and parts of Europe.

Their church planting in underdeveloped areas of India and Pakistan has led to the need for solid Biblical training, therefore opening an opportunity to establish an Associate Degree Bible and Christian Ministry program currently used at their mission points in three areas of India, Pakistan and as of March 2009, the Philippines. Writing and teaching are two of their God-given gifts, and these have served them well in developing classes and teaching in these Bible Schools and the Church at large, in both domestic and international fields – and also in the writing of other books and teachings for edification of the Body of Christ over the years.

Finally, in 2007, Janice was able to retire from a 35 year nursing career in answer to her prayer of 1991, moving into full time work with the mission organization, as well as her love of writing, editing and publishing. Janice has Bachelor of Science in Nursing, and Master of Ministry degrees. This book has been her greatest delight, because she is now convinced, "every woman needs a heroine." New frontiers are on the horizon for 2009.

Some other books offered by

Preparing the Way Publishers

Bridging Two Worlds: Communicating God's Heart to Today's World. (A handbook on the function and operation of prophetic ministry in the Church) By Dave Woodrum....$13.95

The Current Global Reformation and its Effect on the World Missions Movement (A close look at today's radical paradigm shift back to New Testament Church life and missions) By Dave and Janice Woodrum $10.95

The Church Triumphant at the End of the Age (A complete reference of Church history, revivals and restorations, Church today, and reaching the great harvest before Christ's return) By Nate Krupp with Janice Woodrum..............…........... $12.95

Woman – God's Plan, not Man's Tradition (In depth study of what the Bible really says about women in Church life and ministry) By Joanne Krupp………………………………………….. $11.95

Imitate Me As I Also Imitate Christ (Study of discipleship at the highest level, beginning with the example of the apostle Paul) By Dave Woodrum…………………………………….......... $ 8.95

Hope to Hear Soon (Longing and learning to hear the voice of God's heart in the best of times and the worst of times) By Janice Woodrum…………………………………….. $ 6.95

Meet Me in the Garden in the Morning (A guide to deep marital intimacy in communion with God in the mornings)…….…... $ 2.75

Preparing the Way Publishers
411 Zandecki Rd., Chehalis, WA 98532
hojspm@juno.com,

www.PTWpublish.com

(Prices quoted December 2008, please inquire for current pricing.)

ABOUT THE COVER

I would like to extend my sincere gratitude to the Alaska State Government for the use of this handsome photo from their extensive Photo Gallery, showing Governor Palin and boys Trig Palin and Steve Wrigley, at the Alaska State Fair, fall of 2008.

And to Steve Wrigley, thank you so much for posing with the Palin family for this photo. In this case, "a picture says a thousand words." May the Lord bless your life in every way and expand your areas of influence for the good.

The credit for the excellent graphic design of this cover goes to our son Steven Woodrum. We are so proud and pleased to see your work in print!

AUTHOR'S POST SCRIPT

As a result of minor publication obstacles and an intervening international mission trip obligation, the final printing of this book has been delayed several weeks beyond our expectation.

And it seems that in the interval we are able to read the signs of the times more clearly, as we notice a continuous increase in natural disastrous weather patterns and conditions in America. Today we have been told that in a few hours the interstate highway several miles from our home will be closed due to severe flooding – a repeat of unusual conditions we had here (about 30 miles south of Olympia, Washington) only 13 months ago. Several other roads nearby have also been closed due to flooding and mud slides. One contributing factor has been the sudden melt of a 17 inch cumulative snowfall over 10 days (normal snowfall for this area is about 6 inches per year). This has been followed by days and nights of heavy rains. Neighboring farms and businesses are bracing themselves at the thought of repeating the disaster they have just barely recovered from at a terrible price. Similar nearly catastrophic conditions and "natural" disasters are reported nationwide with increasing frequency. We sense the judgments of God are indeed being released in our nation.

Is it too late for America? As I just re-read the story of Noah a few minutes ago, the CD player in another room coincidentally played the phrase, "When the rain starts falling, it's too late; it's too late" of a song by Misty Edwards, from the International House of Prayer, KC, MO. Too late? Maybe ... maybe not.

My husband, Dave, and I have pondered seriously why we are so urgently motivated to get the message of this book out to the public. We recognized in the Spirit that a primary target audience is PRO-LIFE groups across America. We commend you for your years of fighting the hard fight in an uphill battle against abortion in America. Thank you for staying with the arduous battle. We hope this small book will help you know your courageous struggle is greatly appreciated, and our deep desire is that this model family's story will give you a "jump start" to continue the battle with renewed vision, hope and vigor.

And secondly, we target the Christian families who face adversarial and hostile moral climates at every turn, and struggle to make difficult God-fearing decisions in an atmosphere of antagonistic values, corruption and violence such as there was in the days of Noah (Genesis 6:11-13). We pray that the Palin family's story will give you renewed determination and courage to "do it God's way" in all the moral challenges and decisions you may come up against today. And may you see in the life of this family the truth that the fear of God, coupled with hard work and faithfulness can change the course of history for the better. We can make a better world!

Thirdly we challenge church and ministry leaders to return to and adhere to the clear standards found in God's holy Word. Enough of this compromise of its high standards, in order to fit in with the society surrounding us!! Embrace and hold fast to the moral values and standards of excellence in God's Word. Provide a sharp and true plumb line that the Holy Spirit is able to endorse and empower with His gifts and anointings in the Church, our communities and our nation.

Fourthly, we challenge young and older women everywhere who may experience an "untimely" pregnancy, to choose two rights, enduring 9 short months so another person can "have a life." And may we all commit ourselves to look more steadily at the Lord Jesus and His ways, seeking to walk "against the flow" of a deteriorating society, so we may truly be His bright beacons of light in a dark and stormy world. Young families, buckle up! Grandparents, walk close alongside! Church families, walk a tight moral path; stick together and hold tight! We can still make a difference in our society and the world.

Even in the midst of adversity, may we hear all the more clearly God's still small voice saying, "This is the way; walk in it" (Isaiah 30:20-21). And lastly, to echo Sarah Palin,

"God bless ya!"

Printed in the United States
136975LV00003B/6/P